Hope you'll
take the time to
read + reread this,
To me has much the same
info as the DPM but from
a different point of view,

Rich

# Transactional
## Analysis
### for
## Moms and Dads

**WHAT DO YOU DO WITH THEM
NOW THAT YOU'VE GOT THEM?**

# Transactional Analysis Analysis for Moms and Dads

## WHAT DO YOU DO WITH THEM NOW THAT YOU'VE GOT THEM?

**MURIEL JAMES**

Human Relations and Communications Consultant

Lafayette, California

▲ ADDISON-WESLEY PUBLISHING COMPANY

Reading, Massachusetts • Menlo Park, California

London • Amsterdam • Don Mills, Ontario • Sydney

Other books authored by Muriel James:

*Born to Love: Transactional Analysis in the Church*
*Techniques of Group Treatment with Transactional Analysis* (to
be published Winter of 1974).

Books coauthored with Dorothy Jongeward:

*Born to Win: Transactional Analysis with Gestalt Experiments*
*Winning With People: Group Exercises in Transactional Analysis*
*Transactional Analysis for Secondary Students* (to be published
Spring of 1974).

The above are all published by Addison-Wesley Publishing Co.,
Reading, Mass.

Cartoons by John Trotta

Second printing, April 1974

ISBN 0-201-03276-7
BCDEFGHIJ-DO-798765

To My Mom and Dad . . .

And to all the other Moms and Dads who *do* their best, then figure out ways of doing even better . . .

And to all the Moms and Dads who *don't* do their best,

but *can*

and *are*

willing to do better . . .

I salute you!

Muriel James
Lafayette, Calif.

# Foreword

This book is a gift. It is a gift of love to those who feel children are important. In it, Dr. Muriel James shows her love, fun, warmth and understanding as she tells parents—even tired parents—how to help their children learn workable ways to live every day. She does this by teaching parents how to be good to themselves also. In a thoroughly practical way, she demonstrates this because she has been there herself. Instead of telling parents what to do and not to do, in cookbook fashion, she repeatedly asks them to think in new ways—and she shows how to do this.

Rearing children is a tough job. We know, we've been there too. Though we are both psychiatrists, rearing our four children has been rewarding but not always easy. We wish we could have had this book years ago, since it shows how child-rearing can be more fun and less struggle for both parents and children.

We believe that those who are responsible for children will use this book to help them to more joy in living and loving.

Read it. And, as Muriel says, "Think about it."

Doctors Lillian and John O'Hearne

# *Acknowledgments*

To my own children and the many others I have parented—and to those who have lovingly parented me—my thanks.

To Dr. Eric Berne, Dr. Kenneth Everts, and the many members of the International Transactional Analysis Association from whom I have learned so much and who have been willing to learn from me, my thanks.

To Joyce Rosdahl, who suggested the title, and to the staff of Addison-Wesley, whose interest helped bring this book into reality, my thanks.

To Drs. Lillian and John O'Hearne, for their very gracious Foreword, my thanks. They are beautiful, intelligent parents of four lovely children. Both are also psychiatrists in private practice and teaching members of the International Transactional Analysis Association. Lillian has served as consultant to juvenile court and to Hilltop Home for Delinquent Girls, both in Kansas City, Missouri. John is Clinical Professor of Psychiatry at the University of Kansas Medical Center and is President of the American Group Psychotherapy Association. I treasure their friendship.

*Lafayette, California*                                    Muriel James
*January 1974*

# Contents

# Different Strokes for Different Folks

## Chapter 1

You're sound asleep. It's Sunday morning. You'd hoped to catch up on some needed rest. The bed is warm and cozy and the dream that you're just waking up from was lovely. Suddenly a plate crashes in the kitchen. Little Billy screams, "She made me do it!" You struggle out of bed, inwardly moaning, "Oh, no, not again! Not today! I just don't think I can take it anymore."

But you do take it, as you have time and time again. Furthermore, you dish it out on occasion, though sometimes not in the tender, loving way you think would be good for the children. Of course you know that taking it and dishing it out doesn't solve the problem. The kids still fight over the breakfast cereal, your stomach still churns with frustration, and some days nothing seems to change for the better, only the worse.

You turn over in bed, pull the blanket over your ears and try to ignore the squabble in the kitchen. You begin to wonder about yourself, your spouse, your kids. You fantasize walking out. You find yourself thinking, "What's it all about?" or "Is this all there is?" or "Is the whole mess worth the struggle?"

You drag yourself out of bed and down the hall to the kitchen. "Hey, kids," you shout, "Why don't you pipe down so I can sleep awhile. All week I work hard, and on Sunday I need a little peace and quiet. I can't take it anymore when you're so noisy."

You look around the kitchen. It's a mess. Evidently your 12-year-old was up during the night, fixing toast and peanut butter. It looks like he fixed a lot of it; there are crumbs and sticky knives and plates all over.

Evidently he dropped a coke and let in the dog—who had muddy feet—and tried to mop it all up but didn't quite succeed. And you've told him over and over again, "Clean up the kitchen after you mess it up." You'd like to wake him and shake him and bawl him out, but yelling at the younger ones is upsetting enough and there's a chance your 12-year-old would retort with one of those new words he's learned from the neighborhood kids and you just don't feel like dealing with that now.

And that's the way it feels some Sunday mornings. Sticky and crummy! ✿

So what to do about it? That's the question you keep asking yourself all week. In your head you can hear an internal dialogue running on and on. The dialogue is filled with parental comments like your parents used to make, such as, "You should be more patient," and child-like responses like you used to make when you were little: "But I can't," or "But I won't."

The point of this book is to show you that you can. That it really is possible to appreciate your young children—even when you're worried, tired, or sick; even when they're disobedient, bratty, or sick.

This book will show you specific ways of coping constructively on the bad days and specific ways of getting mileage out of the good days. It will help you understand your family because it deals with many typical family problems. I've also included some autobiographical material, as I felt like sharing myself with you and hoped you might be interested. I've written this in an imaginary dialogue form. Hopefully it will reflect some of the questions you would have asked or statements you would have made.

Do you recall any of the fairy tales you used to hear as a child? One of the themes was that of the handsome young prince who had fallen under an evil spell and been turned into a frog. He was doomed to remain a frog until someone, out of loving kindness, would kiss him and restore him to his original form. Well, according to Transactional Analysis, which is the basic theory to be used in this book, every child is born to be a little prince or little princess. Unfortunately, childhood experiences may cast their own version of an evil spell and make many people feel like frogs instead. On certain days, if things go wrong, even *you* may feel that way. On other days, if things go really wrong, even you may *act* a little froggy. And be mad at yourself for doing so. And swear you'll never do it again. And then another nasty day comes when you lose control again. And get mad at yourself again. And again swear you'll not do it. And then you do. Once more you're caught up in frogginess. "Damn it," you say to yourself.

Well, it takes a bit of positive stroking to change any frog back into the prince or princess it was meant to be. 🐸

*"Stroking?"* you ask, *"What's that, Muriel?"*

Good question. There are two kinds—positive and negative. Positive stroking is some kind of touch or other form of recognition like a smile or a greeting. Negative stroking is some kind of unfriendly touch or other form of recognition such as a frown or a critical remark. Stroking is one of the most important things a parent can do for a child.

*"Well, I stroke my kids plenty, Muriel. If they stick a hand in the cookie jar before dinner I give them a hard stroke on the bottom, where it'll do the most good."*

No, I don't mean that kind of stroking. If given often, that kind of stroking may lead to the development of a frightened froggy child. A froggy child may act obedient, even "nice," but do so out of fear rather than out of inner self-direction.

*"OK, OK, but how can I get the kids to mind? When I was little my folks yelled at me and beat me sometimes and I learned to be careful, to shut up, and avoid them."*

Is this the way you want your kids to feel about you?

*"Well, no. I like my kids, at least most of the time. I want to be friends with them. I want things different between us than between my folks and me. And they are. And I want them to be even better."*

I believe you, so here's how to start. Learn about what makes people tick. Think of your personality as being in three parts—the Parent, Adult, and Child. Eric Berne, founder of Transactional Analysis (TA), said that at any time people could act from any of those personality parts, which he called ego states. People acting from their Parent ego state would copy the ways their parents acted. Or they could act from their Child ego state, as they wanted to act or were trained to act when they were children. Or they could act from their Adult ego state, like a logical, thinking person. The ego states can be diagrammed using P for the Parent ego state, A for the Adult ego state, and C for the Child ego state.

Each person's ego states are somewhat different, of course, but typical comments in two people that reflect their ego states could be like those in the figure below. ✤

Any time something new enters the environment a person can flip ego states. For example, if you're sleeping soundly and are wakened by a crash of dishes and argument in the kitchen, you're likely to flip ego states. First, your Child ego state is likely to feel resentment for being disturbed. Then if your Adult starts functioning, you're likely to evaluate the noise and decide whether or not it's important and needs your attention. If your Parent gets "hooked," then you'll act as your parents would have acted in a similar situation. This may be critical and punitive or nurturing and protective.

Let me give you an example of how I sometimes flip ego states. When I was little, I was taught to curtsy to my father's associates if they were older and if he admired them academically. Imagine curtsying!! When I was about ten years old, my Adult ego state concluded that this was archaic behavior. "No one does it and I don't want to," I said to my father. He agreed. So I stopped curtsying *externally*. But internally I didn't. To this day when I meet someone who is older (and that's getting harder every day) and whom I admire academically (and that's also getting harder*), I have an almost involuntary reaction. Something in my head and body seems to respond to an invisible nod from my

---

*Don't misunderstand. I like many people in the academic world, but as I get older I find myself being a little thriftier with my admiration than when I was very young and impressionable.

father. Once more I see him looking at me over the rims of his glasses and nodding to indicate that it's time to curtsy. And I feel like one of those rubber bulbs in the back of a toilet tank that goes up and down when the handle is moved. My curtsy doesn't show outside but I sure do feel it inside. And that's a flipping of ego states.

And that's the way it is. Whatever you teach your children—whether to automatically curtsy or to think for themselves—it will all contribute to the development of their frogginess or their prince and princess traits.

Now I'm not going to tell you never to get angry, or
sad, or hurt, nor am I going to try to get you to be
"perfect" parents. That wouldn't be realistic at all.
You and your feelings are important, just as important
as your children and their feelings. Part of being a real
live person is risky because it sometimes involves making
mistakes, offering apologies, and trying to correct situations you may have messed up. But parents who use
their Adult ego states to think about their children are
willing to do those things. I'm guessing that you're one
of them and I'm glad.

*"OK, Muriel, and thank you. But what about that
Sunday morning hassle when I want to sleep? Got any
ideas about what'll work on that?"*

Well, maybe nothing will work. But maybe something
will. I remember feeling the same way you do when my
children were young. So I let them stay up an extra
hour past their usual bedtime on Saturday night. Then
after they were asleep I'd put some juice and graham
crackers beside their bed. This would often give me
extra sleeping time in the morning. One of my friends
used the technique of "Sunday" toys. After her children were asleep she would put out specially well-
liked toys that were played with only on Sunday. She
said it really worked.

Of course, if we're talking about babies who are too
young to get out of a crib and play, you'll need to adjust
the suggestions for their age. An extra bottle to sip on?
A new mobile to watch? A daytime nap for you when
the baby is asleep?

If we're talking about school-age children who are old enough to make some rational decisions and take responsibility for themselves, you'll need to plan further. The best plan is to tell them carefully the night before what you expect of them; for example, that they are to play quietly until 9 A.M. Then, if they do so, give them a positive stroke. Say something like, "I really appreciate your being considerate this morning," or " I feel so good with the extra sleep. Let's go on a picnic."

Positive strokes can be conditional or unconditional. Children need both kinds. They need unconditional strokes like "I'm glad you're you" just because they're real, alive little people. They need conditional strokes such as, "If you get your room cleaned up regularly, I'll be happy and you'll get your allowance," because this kind of conditional stroke helps develop good habits and manners. ✄

Princes and princesses are attractive. They have good habits and manners and are pleasing to be around. They treat themselves and others with respect. Frogs are the opposite. But people are not meant to be frogs. Positive stroking allows a person to shed froggy ways.

I don't mean that frogs are not OK. As frogs they're fine—they help keep the ecological balance, their croaks are pleasant to other frogs, their swimming kick has been copied by Olympic stars, and they are considered (by some people) to be a delectable epicurean delight.

But people are not frogs; people are people born to be princes or princesses unless early experiences convince them that they are frogs. If that's the way they feel, the process can be reversed. Boys and girls—and moms and dads—can cast off the froggy skin and take up the interrupted task of becoming who they were meant to be. ❧

Incidentally, when you look at yourself in the mirror, what do you see? And when you look at your children, do you ever see the tiny crowns upon their heads? If you don't, then look again. They'll be looking to you for strokes of love, fun, and companionship, so don't hold back. Hug them, play with them, go places with them, and they're likely to turn into princes and princesses.

You can also avoid doing those things that may cast a spell on them. For example, your children may watch a lot of TV. If so, what kind of programs do they, or you, select? Are they imaginative cartoons, the kind that are funny and fun? Are they exciting adventures, the kind that are challenging and creative? Are they soap operas, the kind that are redundantly rubbish and futilely froggy? Take a period of time and sit with your children in front of the TV. Ask yourself in what way the programs help or hinder their development into princes and princesses.

Also, observe what you read to them frequently. Especially the fairy tales and children's stories, which always carry hidden messages. One little girl often heard:

> "Fi, fi, fo, fum,
> I smell the blood of an Englishman.
> Be he alive or be he dead,
> I'll grind his bones to make my bread."

For years she had nightmares as she identified with the one whose bones would be ground up. And each morning when she awoke, she was unable to do anything until she had selected a hiding place where she could go if necessary. It was a frightening experience. Now, as a grownup, she often wakes up anticipating a frightful experience and plans how to hide from it if it happens. 🪰

It is hard to reprogram a Child ego state in a grownup, but it can be done. It's easier if you start now with your children. So if you scare them, even in "fun"—stop! If you ridicule them, if you are sarcastic even in "fun"—stop! If you lie to them, even in "fun"—stop!

(One of my more painful childhood memories is of being stung on my eyelids by a wasp. My eyelids became very swollen and my father took a picture of me like that. The really painful part is that he later showed it to a group of his friends, who laughed. To me it felt like ridicule and to this day it "hurts" to have my picture taken.)

The kind of stroking children get from their parents
influences the basic positions they take about themselves and other people. If the mother is healthy during pregnancy; if the birth is relatively normal; if the
child is wanted, loved, and cared for properly after
birth; if nothing too traumatic happens in the child's
early years; that child is going to have a life position
of I'm-OK. This child will also conclude that other
people are OK, that the world is full of princes and
princesses and that he or she is one of them. People
with an I'm-OK and You're-OK position know that
life is worth living.

On the other hand, if things go wrong during pregnancy,
birth or early years, a child having these experiences
might conclude I'm not-OK and other people are OK.
Being born the "wrong" sex and being asked "Why
weren't you a boy?" or being *negatively* compared
with everyone else (i.e., "Why aren't you as beautiful
as your sister?") are two of the experiences that lead
children to take a froggy position of I'm not-OK and
you are OK, and conclude from this that "My life isn't
worth much."

Things can go pretty well during pregnancy, birth, and
early years and a child could conclude I'm-OK and it's
other people that are not. This position is taken if a
child is compared *positively* to others, i.e., "You're
the only one with the brains in this family," or if a
child is brainwashed with parental prejudice about
"those" people—those who live in a certain place,
speak in certain ways, have different color of skin or
different religious beliefs, etc. Children with this train-

ing, who take the I'm-OK and you're not-OK position, may conclude that "My life is of value but yours isn't."

The fourth life position is usually taken by a child for whom many things go wrong. Such a child receives an overabundance of negative strokes—both verbal and physical—from unpredictable, deserting, seriously depressed, or brutal parents. Children with this experience usually have an I'm not-OK and You're not-OK position, and feel that life isn't worth anything at all. 🌿

A TA colloquialism is "Different strokes for different folks." This means that different people like different kinds of strokes and each ego state within a person has different stroke needs. The three ego states mentioned earlier are established by the time a person is two years old, and they can continue to develop throughout life. Your children have a Parent ego state that includes behavior copied from you. You can see it functioning if you watch them caring for their dolls, pets, friends, or family members. Their Child ego state contains the characteristics and abilities they were born with and the training, trauma, and experiences that have happened to them since birth. They also have an Adult ego state able to compute some things at a very early age; a child of one and one-half can tell a truck from a tractor, a cat from a dog, mama from daddy. Helping a child expand his or her Adult ego state capacities is part of good parenting.

Consider the past three days. Which ego states in your children have you stroked? Did you stroke their Adult by encouraging them to think? Did you stroke their Parent by encouraging them to babysit? Did you stroke their Child by encouraging them to have fun?

Which ego state in you did the stroking? Did you say something like, "Wow, you're fun to be with!" (Child to Child). "Gee, I'm so tired, please help me." (Child to Parent). "Do you have enough allowance to pay for the movie?" (Adult to Adult). "Here, let's change the baby together." (Parent to Parent). "You really are a very good girl (boy)." (Parent to Child).

Try drawing lines in this figure from your ego state to the ego states of one of your children and fill in a few details of what you said and did. ✄

You

One of your children

When I was a little girl and asked my parents a question they would reply, "Think about it, Muriel." This did not turn me off. It gave me "permission" to think. It strengthened my Adult ego state by stroking it. After I thought for awhile or looked it up in the dictionary or tried to get information in some other way, I could, if unsure, ask them again for help. I often had the feeling that they would take my questions seriously. This was a fine unconditional stroke. Though my parents were far from perfect, I'm still grateful to them for that permission.

Children model themselves after their parents in many ways. Your children are learning what marriage is like by observing yours. (A later chapter will have suggestions of what to do if the marriage has gone on the rocks.) So another question you might ask yourself is:

You

Your spouse

"How did I stroke my spouse in the last few days? " Which ego state in you said or did what, and to which ego state in your spouse? Was it a positive, affirming stroke that enhanced his or her self-esteem? Draw lines and put in brief details in the figure at the left.

Please, now, think of yourself. You are important. How about your own need for positive strokes? Do you need to stop doing something and/or start doing something else so that each of your ego states gets recognition? If so, what do you need to do? Are you using all of your ego states to give to others the many lovely things you can give? And to get for yourself the many lovely things you need? Each ego state has value for turning frogs into princes or princesses. Think about it!

# Contracting
## for
## Strokes

## Chapter 2

You've spent your day off cleaning out the garage, weeding the garden, and babysitting the kids. You're hot, tired, and sweaty. You'd like a nap but your spouse has gone gallivanting somewhere and the children are so young they need your attention. You sit down with a cold drink and the dialogue in your head begins again. The Parent in you is critical because you are stopping before you get some painting done. The Child in you is feeling a bit guilty. The Adult listens to the inner argument but isn't functioning at that moment so it can't referee between the other two parts.

Just then your spouse comes in laden down with packages, collapses in a chair and complains, "I'm so tired from shopping I don't want to cook dinner. You watch the kids some more and get the barbeque started while I soak awhile in a hot tub and relax."

Fireworks go off in your head. You feel as if you'll explode. Look how hard you've been trying all day and no one appreciates it! Even the kids didn't thank you when you got them an ice cream bar from the man with the ice cream truck. You bottle up your anger against your spouse, but get crabby with the kids. Suddenly your old ulcer begins to make itself known.

*"Well, for Pete's sake, Muriel, how could I feel different at a time like that?"*

Well, maybe you couldn't. But you don't know until you try something new. The something new is learning how to make contracts—with yourself, your children, and your spouse. ❧

A contract, in transactional analysis, is an agreement to change something.[2]

Contracts can be made about many different things—about changing behavior (i.e., to play with the children instead of yell at them), about changing attitudes (i.e., to be glad, instead of envious, when the kids get a big present from your ex-spouse); or about changing psycho-somatic symptoms (i.e., to learn to relax and admit to being angry instead of denying it and getting ulcers).

To make a contract you must be first aware that whatever's bothering you *is* a problem that needs to be solved. You must then decide to *do* something about the problem. This decision is a basic commitment to yourself and/or to someone else to make a change.

Contracts need to be realistic and potentially achievable. Furthermore, they need to be stated in simple, child-like language, with specific steps to take to affect the changing.

You can make contracts with yourself or with others. For example, you can make a contract with *yourself* to work less and take more time off just to have some fun. Or you can make a contract with your *spouse,* to go out at least twice a month for fun, with each of you taking responsibility for planning one of the occasions. Or you can make a contract with your *children,* to keep all their clothes picked up for one week in return for a special treat. ❧

The reason so many parents have what they feel are un-
solvable problems is because they discount the problem
or themselves in some way.  To discount something is to
make something cheaper than it really is.  A common
discount is to say something like "Well, I can't do anything about it."

There are four ways people discount problems:  by
discounting the problem itself, by discounting the importance of the problem, by discounting the possibility
of solving the problem, or by discounting one's own
ability to help.[3]

Many parents discount their children's problems.
Suppose, for example, that a ten-year-old does not get
invited to a neighborhood party.  That can be an important issue to the child, but a parent might discount the
problem with, "Well, you have plenty of other things
you can do," or discount the importance of the problem
with, "Now honey, it really doesn't matter all that
much," or discount the possibility of solving the problem with, "Well, nobody can make them invite you, you
know," or discount his or her own ability to help with,
"I'm sorry you didn't get invited, but there's nothing I
can do about it."

But discounting is a way to avoid problems, not to solve
them. ✤

*"That's well and good, Muriel, and I wish I didn't lose my temper with my kids. But I do, even when I decide not to. So what about that? Does that mean I'm discounting my own ability to control myself?"*

Well, what do you think? If you've made contracts and didn't keep them, it's probably because you made them either with your Parent, who didn't stick by what he or she said, or with your Child, who promised but didn't keep his or her word either.

It's not enough to say, "I will stop doing something," such as yelling at the children. If you stop something negative, there will be a vacuum unless you put something positive in its place. You need to say, "I will do something else instead." You could make a contract, for example, to "count to ten" *instead* of exploding, or to sit down and tell your children why you are angry and what you expect them to do. Don't say, "I wish you would . . . " Wishing sounds as if it comes from a Child ego state. Instead, speak from your Adult and say, "I expect you to . . . " If you add the words, "Are you willing to do it?" the response will be surprisingly positive. Your children may think of you as a prince or princess because you are treating them with respect. You are their models, for better or worse. Using contracts will make both of you better.

*"Well all right, I can see that if I get contracts out of the family things might be smoother, but what about me? How do I get my needs met? What can I do to get the kind of stroking I want?"* ❧

What kind of stroking do you want? Do you want to be stroked for appearance? For achievement? If so, what kind? And from whom do you want strokes? From a lot of people? From a few? From your boss? Your spouse? Your children? From a stranger you pass on the street? Just exactly what do you want them to say or do so you will feel stroked?

Now the next problem is: What will you need to do to get the strokes you want? How will you need to change your behavior? And then, what will you do after you get your strokes? I overheard two young teenagers the other day. One said, "Oh, I'd die if anyone told me I was pretty." The other said, "Oh, but you are." The first one turned to her angrily and yelled, "See what you did! You gave me a stomach ache by saying that!" People who get good strokes when they expect bad strokes hardly know what to do with them.

Most people are "stroke hungry," and strokes are almost as necessary for health as food and water. Many examples have been recorded of infants who die because they don't get enough strokes. You know, of course, that solitary confinement for prisoners is considered a painful punishment because the prisoner is then in a situation where he gets almost no strokes from others.

For children, being sent to one's room for extended periods of time is similarly painful. Without enough strokes children of any age become apathetic and their physical and emotional development may be retarded.

Therefore, make a contract to give more positive strokes. Tell your children two encouraging or complimentary things each day. Your children will blossom in new ways if you do. Say "yes" oftener than "no," say "do" oftener than "don't."

*"Meaning what?"*

Well, I remember one contract I made with myself and my children that was so important it actually changed our whole relationship. The contract was to say "yes" instead of "no" whenever I thought a "yes" might be possible. I made this contract at a time in my life when I was raising the children, going to school, and, by necessity, working. I was overly tired and was saying "no" far too often. So I told the children that instead of an automatic "no," I would "think about it"; then, if they didn't beg, I would perhaps say "yes." And that's the way it turned out. The "yes's" greatly increased in number and so did our happiness.

*"I get that, Muriel, now what about the do's and don'ts?"*

Whereas all parents need to influence their children, their instructions can have at least four interpretations: What the parents say they mean, what they really mean, what the literal meaning is, and what the children think they mean. Suppose, for example, mom or dad says, "Don't hit your little sister." If asked, mom or dad would say that that means not to hurt little sister. They might *really* mean "Be quiet," but their literal meaning is "Don't *hit* sister." What a child could think they meant is, "Don't hit little sister. That's what they said. But they didn't say not to kick her." Or if a child picks up the unspoken "Be quiet" message, he may just wait until mom or dad are out of the room so they won't hear sister crying, then hit, kick, or bite her.

As another example of why don'ts don't work, think of children who hear a lot of "Don't play with those kids across the street." They may take this literally to mean they can't *play* with them but then conclude they can fight with them instead.

*"Well, that's kind of tricky, Muriel. If I don't say don't, what do I say?"*

Say "do" instead of "don't." Do use positive statements whenever possible instead of negative statements. Do say something like, "Cookies are for *after* lunch or dinner. Carrots or apples are to eat *before* lunch or dinner." Do say, "Treat your little sister gently and you will both have more fun." Do accept some of your children's "don'ts." ❧

There is often a natural healthy rebelliousness in children when they say "don't." It shows in such situations as when they kick off blankets that are too tight or when they fight back if being attacked. The unhealthy rebelliousness, which many parents call brattiness, is the way children learn to act if they have parents who are brutal, overindulgent, or inconsistent.

With brutal parents, many children feel frightened and angry but often try to hide their feelings out of fear. With overindulgent parents, many children feel powerful when having a rebellious temper tantrum to get what they want. With inconsistent parents, many children discover that if they whine and beg they stand a 50–50 chance of either being spanked or getting what they want. And those odds are good enough so they'll try it.

What kind of strokes do your children expect from you? What kind do you expect from them? Are you discounting the importance of strokes in any way? For example, are you discounting your children's need to hear you say "I love you" by being too busy? Or are you discounting the importance of this need by saying, "Oh, they're always begging for attention"? Or are you discounting the solvability of this need with, "No words would satisfy them"? Or are you discounting yourself with, "Well, I just can't talk that way"? ✿

Many people have been trained in childhood not to ask for positive strokes. They've been trained this way by parents who say such things as, "I'll give it to you when I'm good and ready, so don't ask." Many have also been programmed with comments such as "Don't say that to them or they'll just get conceited." They may also have been trained to reject strokes given to them, trained with comments such as, "You can't trust anyone." When grown up, such a person might reject a compliment on a well-prepared dinner with, "Oh, the dinner wasn't that good," or "I know you didn't really mean that." Or they'll accept only half a stroke and reject the other half, e.g., "Well, the meat was good, but the dessert wasn't quite right."

Everyone has different stroke needs because everyone has different ego states.[4] Moms and dads with their different stroke needs and different ways of giving strokes may not know what their spouse wants. Mom may hope to be told that she's beautiful or a good thinker or a good mother, etc. Dad may hope to be told that he's strong and handsome, or good at solving problems, or a fine provider. A contract to tell each other of one's own stroke needs and to try to meet the stroke needs of others is life-giving for those involved. It is also good education for the children who observe it.

Everybody needs an imaginary stroke bank[5] where they save up some of the goodies they've been given, the warm compliments and the loving touches. Then on a day when things go wrong, as they sometimes do, the strokes in the bank can be drawn on and the memory of the good things once said make the bad days much better. ❧

You can make stroke contracts to tell people what you want in specific situations. Not hint for what you want, but actually tell them. Say things such as, "I want you to tell me I look nice, will you?" or "I want you to compliment me for cutting the lawn so well," or "If you think I had a good idea, then please tell me."

You'll need to think about the specific kind of strokes you want, of course, because one type of stroke may take different forms for different people. For example, when I was a little girl, if I had a cold, my parents would bring me English muffins and applesauce. I developed a real passion for them, probably because I liked the concerned attention that went along with the food. I may even have developed a cold or two to get it. Applesauce and English muffins were nurturing strokes to the Child in me.

I seldom get a cold now, but when I do I usually get those special things from my childhood. But there was a time that I didn't get them—because I didn't ask for them. My husband would automatically bring me what was brought to him, namely ice cream and gingerale. A good friend would bring me tea and toast, which is what was given to her. Both were acting from *their* Parent ego states with behavior copied from their own parents. So I made a contract with myself and them to ask specifically for what I wanted—not hint, but ask. And now the rare cold means tasty—and comforting—applesauce and English muffins for me. Asking directly is the Adult ego state, acting like a good parent by recognizing the OK desires of the child and finding ways of meeting the desires. 🐸

The Parent in my head has different stroke needs. Like my mother and father, it wants children to do well in school and to politely say thank you when given something. One of my current activities is as director of a small private school for teenagers who are turned off or who function poorly in over-crowded public schools. Once in awhile this part in me, my parent, feels not-OK around these teens. When it does, I talk to them and ask them if they are willing to say "thank you" a little more often to me and to the rest of the staff. I also ask them what kind of school changes are necessary so that they can do better with their academic work and social adjustment. (After all, my actual parents wanted, and now the Parent in my head wants, people to "think about it.") The students' responses are always interesting and the Parent in me feels stroked with the increased "thank you's" and improved school work.

My Adult ego state has few stroke needs. Although it welcomes a stroke of recognition from a peer for a job well done, it seems to stroke itself for logical data processing. It's been interesting to me to discover that if I don't use my Adult for awhile, I begin to feel a little rusty. I need new input, new problems to solve, new ideas to think about. Evidently using my Adult keeps it well-oiled, well-functioning, and well-stroked. I like that. Currently I'm using my Adult to decide what to do with the rest of my life. I'm thinking in terms of one year from now, five years, ten years, etc. My stroke needs and my ability to give strokes will no doubt be different. I can use my Adult to do probability estimating, but I can't be sure what the situation will be at that time. One thing I know is that I'll always want strokes and it's up to me to figure out how to get them and make contracts to do so. ❧

*"OK, Muriel, I'm getting the point. Now can we focus in more on families?"*

Well, how about making some family contracts? One of the best is to have a family council meeting at least once a week, at a regular time. You can also make a contract to rotate the leadership. Everyone learns by doing. It's a good stroke to be asked to run a council meeting, but don't expect Roberts' Rules of Order to work with preschoolers.

There are many council techniques. One is to set an agenda with each person deciding what they want to talk about. To be sure that the agenda gets covered, a three-minute egg timer can be used with three or six minutes devoted to each subject. If your children have not learned to tell time, they'll find this particularly fascinating. A variation of this is that a subject can be brought up and each person is entitled to three minutes to voice their opinion.

A favorite technique some families use to keep the air clear is a 20-minute resentment and appreciation session. The procedure for this is to set a contract that everyone will express their resentments while the others listen and not defend or argue. Next each person expresses the appreciations they have for each other. After this comes discussion of the resentments or clarification of them. When the session ends it is often with apologies, agreements, and hugs.

Listening to what children have to say—listening to their words and to the feelings under their words—is one of the finest strokes you can give. To listen is to say, "I see you, I hear you, I respect your ideas and you."

What goes into your mouth at meal time isn't half as important as what comes out of it when family members talk to each other around the table. Therefore, in a family council encourage each person to speak directly *to* the other, and not *about* the other as if the person wasn't there. This sounds simple but it's not. It's easy to blame others but many accusations, such as "She made me do it," or "If it weren't for her . . . ," "He always . . . ," are setups for further arguments and psychological "games." If the accusations are between siblings, mom or dad is often hooked into acting as judge and jury and the game becomes a courtroom.

On the other hand, if children, as well as grown-ups, make contracts to be direct and open, a conversation at a family council or dinner table could go quite differently. Each would speak, each would be listened to, everyone would feel stroked. ❧

Have you ever wondered about the hierarchial privileges
in many families? Ever wondered why parents feel they
have rights to privacy and secrets but children do not?
Yet children need privacy. In the secret corners of their
minds are the fantasies of being froggy or being a prince
or princess. Respect their secrets if you want them to
respect yours. Being respected and respecting others is
a sign of royalty.

Some families are obviously a unit, meaning the members
have the capacity to work together. Families like this
think of themselves as "we" and a lot of mutual positive
stroking goes on between them. However, in many families one or more people withdraw psychologically from
the others. This divides the family into subunits.
Though they may be living together, the "heart" of the
family is not whole. Someone will have a heartache;
someone will be a scapegoat. When this is the case,
both parents need to become aware of it and, sharing
equal responsibility, make contracts to pull the unit
together if possible. Of course there will be problems.
Yours and the children's. That's the way it is. But
whenever children have problems, it's not just the children's problems, it's the *family's* problem. It's everyone's problem.

Sometimes parents overburden their children by talking
constantly about grown-up problems such as job insta-
bility or a friend's serious illness. This may cause children to feel helpless because they are unable to solve
the problem and unable to make mom and dad happy.
They can't solve the problem about jobs or illness because they don't have Adult information or power.

They can't make mom or dad happy because mom and dad's attention is directed elsewhere. In situations like this, children often feel guilty as well as helpless, and feeling helpless contributes to frogginess. Therefore, carry your own burdens, preferably as a team with your spouse. You can do it. ❧

Because problems are something that everyone has at
one time or another, families, as well as individuals,
need to make contracts. Basically, they can contract
to let each other know if a situation is getting tense and
to let each other know before it becomes intolerable.
They can contract to accept each other's feelings without discounting them. They can also contract to dem-
onstrate warmth and affection as often as possible. At
least once a day, by word and by touch.

Although you and your children need to contract for verbal strokes which are strokes of recognition, nothing really takes the place of loving touch strokes. A pat on the shoulder, a caress on cheek or hair, a hug, a kiss, a back rub, a massage are samples of the many ways people can contract for strokes.

There are many forms of massage that feel good. Take foot massage, for example. It seems that many nerves in the feet cause a reflex action in other parts of the body and stimulate circulation. To get this effect, one person sits on a bed or on a chair with the soles of their feet readily accessible. The other person massages the soles, using their thumbs. For a substitute foot massage you can roll a golf ball back and forth under your foot and get a similar stroke effect. Experiment in other ways. See how you feel if you massage your own hands. If simple things like these feel so good and cost not a cent, how about contracting for more of them, in your life and in the lives of your children? You'll be healthier and happier. ❧

The right people, who can give the right strokes, may not always be around to give you what you want, so learning to stroke yourself is a necessary skill. You can make contracts to use your Adult to stroke your own inner Child. You can compliment yourself *unconditionally* just for being yourself, and *conditionally* for your very real achievement. After all, you are trying to be a good parent to your children. Stroke yourself for that. Then when a spouse or a friend isn't around to bring goodies—the equivalent of English muffins and applesauce—you can use your Adult. You can be like a good spouse or a friend to your own inner Child. List the things about you that are OK. Compliment yourself for these OK things. Don't be so critical of yourself. You're not perfect and that's good because if you were you'd be mighty hard to live with. Furthermore, you wouldn't have any friends at all. You *can* take care of your stroke needs, help yourself to overcome frogginess, love and care so much for yourself that you just naturally feel more of a princess or a prince.

You can do the same for your children. Try it. It *feels* good and *is* good. ❧

# Redeeming One of Those Days

## Chapter 3

You're up on a ladder, repairing the gutters before the rain comes. Your wife has gone shopping. The twins are playing quietly and the baby is asleep. It's a pretty good day. Then the phone rings. You rush down the ladder, stub your toe on the door, grab for the phone, and it turns out to be your mother—complaining again.

Or you're fixing dinner. The baby is whining. Your 12-year-old is supposedly out mowing the lawn. Your 10-year-old is muttering angrily as he tries to put a model airplane together. It's hot and sultry and you wish you were swimming but something went wrong with the car and you're stuck in the house until it's fixed. And your husband is out of town on a three-day business trip.

Your mother called long distance earlier in the day and you complained about the heat, the car, and the kids. She was no help. She didn't give you a good stroke by listening to you, only a negative one. She criticized you for complaining, and then complained herself, "Think of all you have to be grateful for. As for me, I don't even have any decent food in the house. Furthermore, it's like being alone here since your father had his heart attack."

"Ok, Mom," you had retorted, "I'm sorry, but can't you ever look at the bright side of things? It's you who's always complaining." And then, feeling worse than before she'd called, you'd hung up the phone and started to cry. A kind of sickish feeling stayed in your stomach most of the day and you knew that neither of you had gotten what you needed—positive stroking that occurs when someone listens, really listens to the words and to the *feelings* that are underneath the words, thinks about them, then responds.

You'd been saving up some negative feelings against your Mom for some time and had at last cashed them in. Your "prize" was feeling misunderstood and crying. Then you stopped to wonder if your mother felt the same.

Collecting feelings is something most people do. They collect feelings of anger, frustration, depression, envy, confusion, etc. when things go wrong. Then, when they have enough feelings saved up, they cash them in, as though they were entitled to some kind of prize—a crying jag, a drinking spree, a temper tantrum, or something of that sort. The bigger the collection, the bigger the prize. Like collecting the little stamps that are given away with groceries, gasoline, and other commodities, the feeling stamps add up.

If a person saves up feelings that are the equivalent of one small book, that person feels entitled to a small prize, such as a temper outburst or crying jag. With a medium-sized collection a person feels entitled to a medium-sized prize, such as quitting something important like school, a job, or a marriage. With a large collection, say a lifetime of saving up negative feelings, a person may feel entitled to commit homicide or suicide.

When a person gets a negative stroke, either conditional or unconditional, that person will collect a negative feeling—a stamp. To discover the feeling stamp you learned to collect, think back to when you were little. Ask yourself what made things go wrong. How did you usually feel when things went wrong? What did you do with your feelings then?

Now think of yourself as you are in the present. What makes things go wrong for you now? How do you usually feel when things go wrong? What do you do with your feelings?

Now consider, is there any similarity between what you experienced and felt as a child and what you feel and experience now as a grownup? If you felt guilty, do you still? If you felt depressed, do you still respond that way? If you felt angry, or confused, or stupid, or inadequate, is that the feeling stamp you still collect? If you do, you don't need to. You *can* feel differently. You *are* trying to be a pretty good parent to your children. And you're reading this because you want to be a better one. Right?

Ok, then I'd like to ask you a question. Do other people control your feelings or do your feelings belong to you? When they feel bad, many people blame others with such statements as: "He spoiled my whole day." "She makes me feel so mad (sad, depressed, confused, etc.)." Of course your feelings are your feelings. They are real, and they need to be recognized and owned up to. But do you know that you can choose which feelings to have? Also, that if you'd like to change some negative feelings, you can? The first step, whether working with your own feelings or those of your children, is to recognize those feelings with comments such as, "You really are mad, aren't you?" Or "You really would like to tell me off. Is that right?" Or "You sound so depressed you must be feeling really down today." And so forth. You can say this aloud to your children or in an inner dialogue, with yourself.

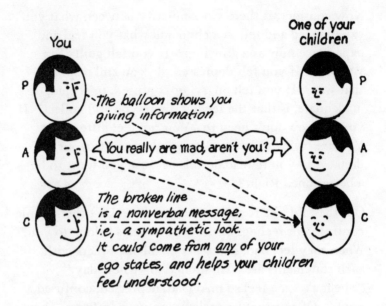

The second step is to ask a question from your Adult:
"How long do you want to feel mad (sad, depressed,
confused, etc.)?" You may get a Child response such
as, "I'm going to feel this way forever (or for a year, or
a month, etc.)."

When taking care of yourself, your Adult can talk
to your own inner child, reflect its feelings and
reprogram the feelings.

If you get a response from your Child ego state, the third step is to ask, "Would you be willing to feel really mad (sad, depressed, confused, etc.) for ten minutes and then give up the bad feeling in favor of a good one?" Recognizing a negative feeling and then putting a time limit on it helps the inner Child feel accepted and safe.

However, the question, "How long do you want to feel mad (sad, depressed, confused, etc.)?" sometimes elicits a response from the Adult instead of from the Child. This Adult response can come even from children, as they too have Adult ego states and can say, "I want to stop feeling this way right now." In this case, the next question is, "What will *you* need to do *now* so you can feel differently?" The "you" implies it's their responsibility, the "now" is a nudge in the right direction. Maybe the answer will be physical exercise, or a new friend, or a new activity. But there is always something you and your children can do to change the bad feelings into good feelings.

*"Oh now come on, Muriel, it couldn't be* that *simple!"*

Oh, but it is. Try it, you'll like it. ⚘

There are many techniques you can use to get in touch with your feelings and then change them.[6] Changing them is like a reeducation process. If your Child ego state has collected a certain negative feeling, your Adult can reeducate it with an inner dialogue. First recognize the current feeling and stay with it a few minutes, then instruct your inner Child to have a different feeling—a positive one.

For example, if you tend to feel depressed because your spouse has to work late, you can recognize the feeling and change it to a feeling of relief or joy by reminding your Child, "Tonight you won't have to cook as much," or "Tonight you can read that book you've been wanting to read (or go to bed early, or go out to a movie, or whatever would please you)." For example, if your children are feeling bad because they weren't invited to a neighborhood party, first sympathize with them: "I guess you're really disappointed." Then help them feel differently, perhaps by saying, "I see you want to be friendly with others. That's great!" Then help them plug in their Adult with, "I wonder if you would be willing to figure out what to do and what not to do so that you'd get more invitations."

If you use this technique regularly when you're feeling bad and about to collect a negative stamp, you will soon find yourself feeling happier more often. The same will be true for your children. The happy feeling is an 18-carat gold feeling. So go for it. ❧

Another technique for dealing with your feelings is to refocus your attention on a different activity. In fact, a common TA slogan is, "If your Child is in control, give your Adult something to do."

*"That sounds good, Muriel. Now what does it mean?"*

What it means is doing something that you didn't do when you were a child and that your parents didn't do either. If neither you nor your parents did it when you were little, then the "something to do" is in your Adult ego state.

For me it was sewing, in the hard years when my children were young and we didn't have enough money. One of my sons had spinal meningitis at age two; another had polio. When my daughter was six she had undulant fever which led to rheumatic fever and other complications. It was during World War II, in the early 40's. Adequate medical attention and the "miracle" drugs that are currently used for those illnesses were not available, and my daughter was in bed for a very long time. Well, they're all grown up and pretty healthy now, but back then I was often very afraid that I wouldn't be able to cope for even one more day. So I learned to sew. I had not been taught to do this as a child, and as my mother didn't sew either, it was an Adult ego state decision and activity. It gave my inner Child temporary relief from problems and pressure that seemed overwhelming. Like a restful vacation that allows a person to return to work feeling stronger, sewing helped me.

Maybe you have had different experiences—either
more or less difficult. In any case, don't do a comparison
trip. Your experiences and feelings are yours and mine
are mine, and each of us has felt overwhelmed at times.
Just as when a tiny bit of gas escapes from a stove it fills
all the space in the room, so problems sometimes seem
to fill all the space in a person's life. But it doesn't
need to be that way.

Each person needs to find the activity for their Adult
that will temporarily turn off their own inner Child.
What will work for one person may not work for
another. For example, when their Child feels overload-
ed, some people find something to read. This works for
them. It doesn't for me. Perhaps because both my
parents read a lot and I also liked to read when I was
little, reading involves all of my ego states. Consequently, reading doesn't turn off my Child. Writing has a
different effect. When I was little I didn't write much,
so now when I do, some older part of me gets activated.
❧

Experiment for yourself. You'll discover something
that will work for you. This is important, because as
a mom or dad your feelings need to be worked with so
that they can be channeled into constructive patterns.
When you do find something that works for you, go on
to experiment with your children. Though you may
not realize it, you already know how to recognize their
feelings and refocus their attention. When your baby
skinned his knee, for example, you probably gave his
knee a few minutes of tender loving care, then read him
a story or got him a toy to play with or somehow di-
verted his attention away from the hurt. It's the same
principle and easy to use.

Some people use meditation, or bodily awareness, or
deep breathing to get in touch with their feelings. Ex-
aggeration of a feeling also works. For example, if you
feel like yelling, plan a time when it won't make others
feel as miserable as you feel, a time when you have privacy, when no one is around. Close the windows and
doors so you won't scare the neighbors, then yell. It
won't solve the problem but it will give you some relief.
You will be able to parent better because you will under-

stand yourself more. I remember many years ago feeling the need to do this so I did, and banged on the wall at the same time and it really helped. I got in touch with the anger I wasn't aware of, but which was activating arthritis in me.

Or if you feel like crying, really cry. Cry yourself ten buckets full of tears. See the buckets in your imagination. See them filling up with tears. Really have at it. Feel really sorry for yourself for the tragedy you have experienced. Cry yourself a river. As you do this you may suddenly find yourself sleepy, so sleep. Or you may start laughing. If you do, then go ahead. Laughing brings six times as much oxygen into the body as does deep breathing. So laugh.

You've probably heard the old cliché, "Laugh and the world laughs with you, cry and you cry alone." Laughing *with* somebody—not *at* but *with*—is a huge positive stroke that will give both you and others that 18-carat gold stamp feeling. Try it tonight as an experiment. It's called laugh therapy and it's great fun. Ask the family if they are willing to experiment with you. If they agree, then start in. Laugh. Even if there doesn't seem to be anything to laugh about, suddenly there will be. Laughter is contagious. Let's spread it around. ❧

Do you want to discover something else new? Want to teach your family about good and bad feelings—how they give them to others and get them for themselves? Then try this if your children are three years old or older. It's an educational technique that will strengthen their Adult ego state.

Get some colored paper and cut it into small squares for feeling-stamps. Use

> gold for those golden good feelings,
>
> brown for those icky bad feelings,
>
> red for anger or frustration,
>
> blue for sadness and depression blues,
>
> green for envy or jealousy, and
>
> white for purity or self-righteousness.

If your children are little, two colors—gold and brown—may be enough. Let each person in the family have an envelope with stamps of each color, or put a bunch of stamps on saucers on a table. Explain what each stamp means. Then ask everyone in the family if they are willing to play this discovery game. If they agree, then select a time period such as 5 P.M. to 8 P.M. Anyone who gets a positive or negative feeling from someone during that period asks that person for a stamp representing the feeling he or she collected. For example, if someone says or does something that makes you feel good (even if he or she doesn't say it to you), then you would collect a gold stamp from that person. At the end of the time period everyone counts their stamps and evaluates their good and bad feelings.

At some other time you may be able to get a contract
with the family to give and receive only these good
gold feelings by giving and getting only positive strokes.
They can be conditional or unconditional, touch or non-
touch.  Try this for a designated time period and see the
princes and princesses that emerge right there, in front
of your very own eyes, in your very own home.  You
can join the fun and be one of them. ❧

# Stroke Needs in Crisis Times

## Chapter 4

You're sitting and reading a good book when the phone rings and somebody tells you that your father, who recently had a serious heart attack, has taken a turn for the worse and to please come to the hospital at once.

You're working in the garden and the school nurse phones to tell you that your child has been hurt and you should come immediately to the school.

You've just come home from a hard day at the office and your spouse greets you with, "I've been thinking about it for a long time, and now I know that I really want a divorce. I'm interested in someone else."

Crisis! Your heart starts to pound, you feel as though you can't breath or move. The sudden, unexpected crisis throws you into a panic and you can't even think straight. Somehow you never believed that something like this would ever happen.

That's the way it is with most crises. They come when we are so ill-prepared that we are often caught up in our own feelings of inadequacy, confusion, tension, anxiety, uncertainty, and apprehension. For example, if you think of your children as bright and interesting, it's not easy to discover that their teacher may think of them as difficult problem children. This kind of situation introduces a *crisis period*, which usually starts with a particular event and extends over a period of time. The crisis period might last until your children have different teachers or until they change their behavior to please their teachers. ❧

"Crisis" is defined as a change or a turning point in a disease, or as a moment of decision. It can be a sudden *unexpected* event, as in the case of an automobile accident, or it can be an *expected* event, such as death after long illness or failing grades after not studying. During any crisis the "stroke bank" may feel depleted and the person involved may feel empty with no resources to draw on. He or she may suddenly feel weak, apathetic, or despairing, instead of strong, active, and hopeful.

Instead of replenishing their stroke bank so they can function better, some people withdraw from the situation or problem; others pretend it doesn't exist and that everything is really fine; still others play the blaming game, attacking other people and refusing to take responsibility. However, some people really get involved in trying to do something positive about the crisis. ✄

*"So what can I do? That's the million dollar question."*

In any crisis it would help if you could possibly count to ten (even if you count quickly). Somehow this gives you a moment of time to plug in your Adult. Then the next thing to do is to ask yourself whether you need to act immediately (as perhaps in the case of getting to the hospital) or you have time to think things through before acting (as in the case of a negative report from a teacher).

If you need to act immediately, then do. Take a few deep breaths, get your car keys if necessary, and get going. If you're driving let your Adult be in control. Be aware that your anxiety may be affecting your normally good judgment. In your head try to think about the immediate situation. Don't let your imagination jump ahead to a possible catastrophe unless, at the same time, you're planning how to avert it.

If an immediate decision is *not* necessary, then you have time to recognize, experience, and deal with your feelings. After you do this you will have the ability to turn on your Adult. Ask yourself, "Is this a crisis I can do anything about or is it out of my hands?" If you decide you can do something about it, then you will need to think through the questions: What? Where? How? When?

*"Good Lord, Muriel, I just can't think during a crisis."*

Yes you can. Really. The *feeling* of not being able to think is a fearful feeling that understandably comes from your own inner Child when faced with a big problem. But don't put yourself down. Your Adult is going to solve the problem, so you might start by giving your Child a little relief from the shock of it all.

You don't think you can? Then experiment with me. Ask your children to take a fun fantasy trip with you. Then slowly read the following to them out loud. Watch their faces.

"Close your eyes and *imagine* that in your hands you have a ripe juicy orange. Hold it, smell it, start to peel it. Slowly peel back the skin and feel the juice running out on your hand. Now break it apart and put a segment in your mouth. Taste the juice as it runs down your throat. Now take another segment as you taste how sweet and juicy it is.

"Keep your eyes closed and imagine you have a lemon. Cut it in two with a knife. Pick up one half, put it in your mouth and suck it."

Now, Mom or Dad, if you were watching your children you probably saw their mouths pucker up. Yes? If imagination can determine what a person *feels and tastes,* then imagination can determine how a person *feels and acts.* Your Adult ego state can determine this.

Turn on your imagination again. See yourself as though caught by a candid camera. See you as you are, faced with a crisis when you're *not* at your best—maybe frightened and inadequate or hostile and ineffective or whatever. Now, in your imagination, look at yourself when you *are* at your best. See yourself as competent, moving through the crisis effectively—hurting maybe, but actually solving the problem. The pictures you can create in your mind doing this fantasy are likely to have validity for you and show your ability to cope with crisis.

After recognizing and admitting to your feelings, after discovering that you really can change them, the next step is to define the crisis clearly. This needs to come before you decide on your possible responses to the crisis. Actually knowing what the crisis is and admitting that it is indeed a crisis will put you miles ahead. Many people deny that a crisis exists or deny the importance of it. Or, if they do recognize it, they act as though it can't be solved or coped with. No matter how painful, it must be dealt with. If not, it will fester and infect from inside. ✄

If the crisis is related to a school situation it may be
necessary for you to get facts from the teacher, the
school psychologist, and your physician. Ask for specific details. Poor sight, poor hearing, poor nutrition
will affect your children's school performance and
social adjustment. Minimal brain dysfunction or emotional trauma will do the same. Over-anxious, over-
nice, over-strict, over-protective, or wishy-washy parents
all contribute to their children's fears and immaturity,
so investigate the crisis from your Adult. Try not to
see the crisis as an insurmountable tragedy, but as a
problem that can be solved.

And of course, if it's about your children and their
school performance, remember, teachers aren't always
right. Who is? I remember being called to school because a teacher of my six-year-old son, who was in the
first grade, said, "His behavior is sexually provocative."
I hurried to school. What in the world could he be doing? "See," said the teacher, "his shirt is unbuttoned
all the time. It's too sexy. And he moves his chest in
and out so it shows." Sure enough, that's what was
happening. The buttonholes on the shirts I had made
for my son were too big and easily came unbuttoned.
It seemed unlikely that the teacher would change her
opinion of what was "sexually provocative," so I told
her I would do something about it. And I did; I made
the button holes smaller and laughingly remembered,
"A stitch in time saves nine." If a few minutes of sewing would stop the teacher from giving negative strokes
to my son, it was worth the effort.

Good teachers help children grow, and lots of them do just that. But occasionally you may meet a teacher who is so critical, demeaning, and prejudiced that he or she is actually destructive to the growth of your children. In this case you could try to get your child moved to another class. Sometimes it works, sometimes not. On rare occasions you might be able to get a teacher fired, but only for some gross, overt action; never for not liking children or for giving them negative strokes. If there is no way out, then try to stroke the teacher for the OK things she *does* do (everybody does *some* good things). Its manipulative, but if it works positively on behalf of your children, why not! ❧

Work *with* the school personnel, not against them, and they are likely to work with you. Some parents do not deal with their children's school problems until the problems seem almost insurmountable. You don't need to be like that. If you had unhappy school experiences yourself, try not to let the feelings in your Child ego state interfere with your capable Adult reasoning power. Children are amazingly flexible. So if you are willing to give yours lots of loving encouragement, setting fair limits on their behavior and realistic goals for their achievement, the prince and princess qualities will emerge.

If the crisis is an accident or an illness involving some-one else in the family, keep in mind that it is primarily *their* crisis. You may need to give intelligent Adult in-formation such as, "You'll have to be in the hospital for three days," and kind, loving, verbal nurturing Parent strokes such as, "I'll think about you a lot and come to see you every day," and kind, loving, nonverbal nurtur-ing Parent strokes such as hugging, holding, gentle squeezes, light kisses, and soft pats. Your Adult can process just what would be appropriate with that partic-ular person in that particular situation.

You will not help a going-to-the-hospital crisis situation by weeping, wailing, and wringing your hands in front of the patient, whether it is your spouse or one of your children. It may only make the person feel guilty and defensive about being sick or injured, or worried and hesitant about revealing his or her feelings. When I say don't weep and wail in front of the patient I do not mean that you should be stoical. Tears to show you

really care are OK, and you may need to give yourself
further relief by turning on the waterworks and crying
ten buckets full of tears when you're alone. However,
it is more helpful if you focus on the feelings of the person who is physically hurting, not on yourself. Then
if you do something so the other person will feel more
comfortable physically and more cared for emotionally,
you'll feel much, much better yourself.

It's scary, being a little kid and going to the hospital.
It's scary thrashing around in bed at home with a real
pain or with a high fever. As a mom or dad, the same
situation may be scary for you. You're likely to need
medical information for your Adult, and both you and
your children are likely to need some extra tender,
loving care. 🌽

Whenever people are sick, anxious, worried, hurt, or tired, their Child ego states become more active than usual. The Child overbalances the other parts of their personalities. And because they're feeling bad they also feel more like a frog than like the prince or princess they were meant to be.

To move yourself out of that feeling, take a piece of paper and write down just what the crisis is. Then draw three big circles for your ego states. Opposite the Child circle write down all the Child feelings you have about the crisis. Opposite the Parent circle write down what each of your parent figures would say and do about the crisis. Opposite the Adult circle write down the facts you already have and the facts you need to get. Your paper might look like the figure at the right.

Now study what you have written down. What part of you is strongest at this moment—and consequently running your life? Is it appropriate? If it isn't, then make a contract for some other way to function. You can do it if you try.

If the crisis is one of death—the death of a parent, grandparent, friend, or pet—what you say to your children is vitally important. Don't say something like, "God's taken Grandma to be with him," unless you want your children to fear God. Do say something like, "Grandma's body got worn out, like an old car, and just wouldn't go anymore." If it's an animal that has died, don't say something like, "Don't worry, we can get another at the pet store tomorrow." Do say something like, "I guess you feel real, real sad that your pet died." If the answer is "Yes," you might add, "Let's have a little funeral so we can talk about him and say goodbye."

Whenever a person experiences the loss of someone they love—whether by death, desertion, or divorce—there is "grief work" that needs to be done. And grown-ups need to do their grief work just as much as children need to do theirs. ❦

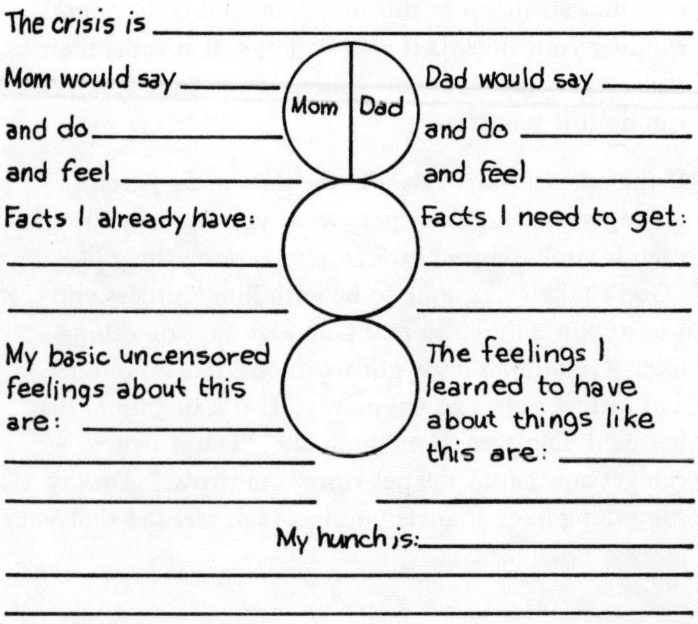

The crisis is _____

Mom would say _____    Dad would say _____

and do _____  Mom | Dad  and do _____

and feel _____    and feel _____

Facts I already have:    Facts I need to get:

_____    _____

_____    _____

My basic uncensored feelings about this are: _____    The feelings I learned to have about things like this are: _____

_____    _____

My hunch is: _____

_____

_____

Grief work has several phases. First, there is shock. Shock may last a few minutes or a few days, and is useful to the extent that, like a temporary anesthesia, it shields us from a reality that we are not prepared to deal with. However, if it continues for some weeks the person in shock may need professional counseling. Sometimes a very few counseling sessions will undo the block. The second phase is when a person comes out of shock. Then he or she may feel the loss is unreal and say things like "I just can't believe it happened," or "It just isn't true."

Next come the strong emotional feelings of grief and loss which need to be expressed, not held back. Then come feelings of loneliness and depression, normal healthy feelings in the process of grief work. One may often experience physical symptoms of distress, such as stomach aches, head aches, back aches, etc. There may be feelings of panic and inadequacy. The feeling of panic may be so extreme that a person fears losing his or her mind. A sense of guilt is usually experienced as well—guilt for doing or not doing something, for saying or not saying something. Frequently this is accompanied by resentment or hostility and the feeling that "someone" should have done something, that "someone" is to blame for what happened. When people are grieving they are so preoccupied that it is often hard for them to get involved with others. If they stay with the process and don't try to block it or stop it, they eventually get their grief work done, establish new relationships, and reexperience the meaning of living.

Death is certainly a major crisis, but children, even
those too young to talk, are affected by any family
crisis. They intuit the unhappiness if one of their parents loses a job, they intuit the bitterness if a divorce is
impending (more about this in a later chapter), they intuit changed relationships if a new baby is born into the
family or if a family member dies. Intuition is a char-
acteristic of the Child ego state, so naturally little children use it to "psych out" the situation. ❧

As soon as children are old enough to understand words, they need to be given facts. This helps them develop an Adult ego state. Then when the day comes that they face a crisis themselves, as they inevitably will, they will have information they can draw on, like money in a bank.

*"OK, I agree with you, Muriel, but will you say it in a sentence?"*

Yes, level with your children by telling them what's going on, how you feel about it, and what you think about it.

Remember, what's a crisis to you may not be one to your children and vice versa. For example, a new job in a new city could seem great to you, but a tragedy to your children if they do not want to leave their friends.

One of the most useful bits of advice I ever heard was in a counseling course where the instructor said that one of the most caring ways to act is "to respect each other's privacy and deal gently with each other's dreams." The respect and gentleness you show to others will help them meet their emergencies with fortitude and courage.

*"But look, Muriel, what if the emergency is happening to me, not to others? What if I were to be told I have a terminal illness?"*

That's a hard crisis to face, but if you can face it with fortitude and courage you will be like a prince or princess and will be treated with gentleness and respect yourself.

*"And what about all those dreams I had of getting married and living happily ever after? I got married but the dreams just haven't come true."*

The hopes and dreams you once had were important. Even now, if the weeks or months left to you are few, they could be thought-provoking vistas toward which you could turn your steps. The daydream comes first, the thinking about it comes next, and the doing something about it follows. If you want to live happily in the time you have left, you can, though it won't be without crisis. You may need to do something differently, change your standards somewhat, accept people as they are, be willing to risk yourself in new ways, but you can be deeply happy and at peace.

These same words apply even if you have many long years of life ahead of you. Either way, would you be willing to think about it?

# None
# But the
# Lonely
# Heart

Chapter 5

You're a parent without a partner. You're alone and you're feeling lonely. In the beginning it wasn't so bad, "Good riddance," you may have thought. "I'd rather make it on my own than with that person." You had looked the landscape over and decided there were some other attractive people giving you the eye. Were they married? Well, yes, maybe, but maybe they were ready for a divorce and available.

You may have thought you were, too—that divorce wouldn't be so tough. Then the realities crept in. You found that your kids are hard to care for when you struggle to work all day, struggle with baby-sitters, struggle with grocery shopping, house cleaning, cooking, etc., etc.

Or maybe you don't have your children except on weekends. And maybe you don't have the house that you worked so hard to buy. And maybe your apartment isn't all that great, especially when the children visit and their toys and friends aren't there. And it just isn't the same at all. It feels kind of artificial to them and you.

Your feelings keep changing. Depressed one day, angry the next, sad, glad, mad in rapid succession. And your "stroke bank" is empty. There doesn't seem to be anything left to draw on. No resources, no nothing. The old question comes back to mind, "What's it all about?" "Is this all there is?"

Maybe you've tried complimenting yourself for trying hard and working hard. Then maybe you've discovered that trying and working hard is really a strain on you and on the people you know—who, maybe, are beginning to avoid you.

You are genuinely fond of your children, but as you observe them they don't seem really joyful. Instead they seem a wee bit frantic or even depressed, as you are.

*"Yeah, that's me, but what can I do? That's the way it is."*

Inwardly you may hear the words of an old song, "None but the lonely heart can know my sadness." Each person has his own sadness, each has loneliness. In the midst of a crowd or even in the presence of family most people sometimes experience the sense of separation, of isolation, of despair. Despair is different from depression. TA teaches that when a person is depressed it is because the inner Parent is being critical and the inner Child is hearing parental criticisms such as "You never do anything right."

When a person is in despair, it is the Adult that is evaluating the situation and saying, "That's the way it really is."

If you are experiencing depression you need to use your Adult to referee between your Parent and Child and to turn off negative Parent tapes. You can do this by giving positive Adult strokes to yourself and to your children.

*"Yes, but what if it's despair?"*

If it's despair, you will need to be courageous and to find new creative ways for dealing with your aloneness.

*"Oh, I once tried one of those clubs for singles. It was terrible. Everybody was trying to find another spouse. Nobody was just trying to get to know each other."*

You tried it once? Or twice? Or a dozen times and
gave up? Why? Maybe it wasn't the right situation.
Maybe you need to relax a little. Meet someone in a
more casual way. For example, you might meet some
interesting people if you were to sign up for a class of
some kind—or take a new job. Or maybe you need to
just get on with living and not put all your eggs in one
basket—another person.

Look around with fresh eyes. If you want a good
parent for your children where might you meet such a
person? Or how about letting your ex-spouse develop
a happy relationship with the children that does not
include the two of you squabbling over child support.
You really can do it. You can give positive strokes to
the OK part of your ex-spouse; you don't need to run
him or her down. You will always demean yourself if

you demean someone else.  Putting down your ex is
hard on the children, too.  Children need parents they
can be proud of, not parents they fear or avoid because
of what one says about the other.

Do something about your loneliness so you don't become bitter.  One of the most important places to start
is with your own physical health and the physical health
of your children.  A few years ago, psychologist A. H.
Maslow developed his theory of the "hierarchy of needs,"
the needs that every human being is driven to realize
and the usual order of their importance.  As you can
see from the figure below, bodily needs are basic; as a
rule they must be met before the others.  So start with
the body. ❧

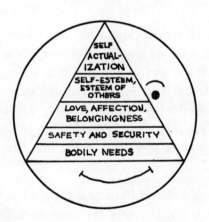

Get yourself and your children an up-to-date, full scale medical checkup—it may save your life or your sanity. For example, a five-hour glucose tolerance test will show whether you have hypoglycemia. Hypoglycemia is easily controlled with diet, but if not controlled it will make you feel depressed and confused and who needs that?

Before you go for a checkup, plan how to aid your doctor. Make a list of any illnesses you or the children have had. List any symptoms, i.e., continuing headaches, joint pains, stomach aches, etc. that you've noticed. Don't be satisfied with a cursory exam; get a blood count, urinalysis, etc. The little Child in you and your children needs to be physically cared for. Start with your doctor.

Even if you get a clean bill of health your body may still need attention. Anxiety and tension drain away needed vitamins and minerals. You may need a strong dietary supplement. Don't just depend on good food to keep your body healthy. Take a course in nutrition

or read some of the excellent books on the subject. It's
hard to think clearly, work hard, and be patient if your
physical self is out of gear. A vitamin B deficiency can
lead to a feeling of isolation. So think about it.

*"Oh wow, Muriel, you sound like my mother or grand-
mother plugging vitamins and diet."*

OK, so maybe I do, but don't turn down the information because you still have a "thing" about them. Don't
let either your Parent or Child undermine your Adult.
I well remember the 1930's and the depression, the
terrible scarcity of jobs and the lack of social agencies
to help out, and the loneliness without a family close by,
and the hunger. That I remember the most—the gnawing,
frightening hunger. I remember tightening my belt until my waist was only 17 inches around, and the deep
hollows in my face, my skinny arms, and not being able
to think well because I was almost starving. I remember
actually stealing a banana one day when I thought I
would faint with hunger. Now I'm glad those days are
past for me and I hope you never experience them—or if
you do, that you find someone like I did. Hope was her
name. She and her husband had never had a daughter
but did have an extra bedroom. It cost $18.00 a month
but there was no charge for the abundant love they gave
me. But back to you.

Your body is important. It's the house you live in so
take care of it. Exercise, rest, and food are vital but
they may not be enough. Read about nutrition and
think for yourself. The library is cheap and so's a
bottle of good vitamins. ✤

Once bodily needs are met, what Maslow called the "safety needs" become important. Without the feeling of safety, children and adults get upset. Children develop a feeling of safety and trust if their parents are fair, consistent, and predictable. Parents who set reasonable limits, and stick to them reasonably well, help their children feel safe rather than insecure and anxious.

But sometimes parents feel that they can't do this. They themselves feel unsafe and may act or feel like insecure children, always being afraid that something terrible is going to happen.

Parents who feel unsafe in their own Child ego states sometimes have an obsessive need for order and try constantly to be perfect themselves and have perfect children. Perfectionist parents, however, like indifferent or inconsistent parents, cause their children to feel unsafe.

If you think you may be stuck at this point of feeling unsafe, then there are many things you can do to reassure your own inner Child. Good locks on the door is one. A reliable friend to talk to is another. Enough money in the bank for an emergency will also help your unsafe feeling. Knowing what community agencies are available for help is also useful.

An important question to ask yourself is "What is the worst thing that could happen?" With this, you may discover that your catastrophic expectations are unreal and therefore nothing to be afraid of. Many moms and dads need to learn how to hang loose. ✿

Hanging loose may involve a contract to stop trying to be perfect (you'll never make it anyway) and be more tolerant of imperfections in yourself and others.  This may mean doing things differently, such as letting dishes sit in the sink overnight instead of insisting that they be done immediately after a meal.  Or letting the lawn get shaggier instead of compulsively manicuring it when you're tired.

It may mean letting the children make some of their own choices (e.g., wearing a green sock with a blue one) or their own mistakes (e.g., spending all their allowance the first day and having nothing left to use later in the week).

On the other hand, if you want your children to feel safer, you may need to be more consistent, not compulsively perfect, but consistent.  You may need to say something and stick with it so that you are more predictable and therefore more trustworthy. ❧

When bodily and safety needs are met, the third need must be met: the need for love, affection, and belongingness. Maslow says, "Love hunger is a deficiency disease like salt hunger or the avitaminoses . . . " This hunger for love is like a "need" for Vitamin C. Without it we are handicapped in some way, feel less strong, less able to cope.

When a family breaks up, the kind of love that is needed to hold the family together is missing. The sense of belongingness is threatened, the unit is split apart—and at least one person with the capacity to give and get some kind of stroking is gone. When the sense of belongingness is missing or is threatened, any person may begin to feel unsafe. His or her body may then experience tension, fatigue, or illness, and the froggy feeling may return.

Everyone needs love and belongingness, so to belong to some kind of a group is important. The small family is one kind of group; people on the job can be another. People with a common interest, i.e., folkdancing, golfing, politics, also feel a sense of belongingness when they are together. The "extended family," a group made up of several families, is a new group concept. (Read about mine in *Born to Love.*) You may need to develop or to join a *loving* group. You can do it. You really can. You need love for yourself. And you need to be able to give love to your children and they need love for themselves. And they also need to be able to give love to others.

Many people, teenagers and grown-ups, mistake infatuation for love. But you know by now that the infatuation you probably felt when you were first married

is not the same as love.  Love is not defensive or posses-
sive.  Love is a trust relation of mutual openness with
an emphasis on positive stroking.  You can be open to
stroking others and to getting strokes.  You can do
something this week so that more love energy can flow
between you and your children.  Will you think about
it? ⚘

Next in the hierarchy of needs are the esteem needs—self-esteem and esteem from others. Esteem is related to feeling confident and capable because of being able to do things. Children need to be encouraged to succeed in things, for this helps develop self-esteem. When they do succeed they also need recognition strokes from others for what they have done. This esteem from others is like strong medicine that enables a child to feel good and get going in even more constructive ways. This get-goingness leads to self-actualization, which is the last in the hierarchy of needs. Self-actualization is the desire to become more and more of what one is, to become everything that one is capable of becoming. Princes and princesses are people in the process of becoming self-actualizing.

If you want this for your children, then love them even though you're lonely and maybe alone. Consider these universal human needs—the needs of the body, the needs for safety, love and belongingness, esteem, and self-actualization. As shown on page 78, these needs appear to be hierarchial, but some of them can interchange. For example, without esteem, a child will feel insecure and may become physically ill. Without affection, a child may eat more or less than his or her body really needs for vitality and health.

Arrange your life and the lives of your children to get these needs met. They are important. So are you. So are your children. And you can do it. ❧

When a parent either with or without a partner is feeling lonely, their "yes's" and "no's" to their children's requests may be arbitrary rather than rational. Children intuit the vulnerability, the "soft spots," in their parents. They learn how to manipulate to get what they want. When little, they may cry, pout, have a temper tantrum, and so forth. At school–age they may try a mild form of emotional blackmail with, "But gee, everyone else has one, why can't I?" or "But gee, everyone else gets to go, why not me?" or "You just don't love me anymore." or "I'm going to run away." or "I'm going to tell __" or "I'll __" or "__" or "__" (you fill in the blanks). You can see through some of their attempts to manipulate you, but not all. ✷

To be more aware of what's going on between you and your children, ask yourself the question, "Is she or he trying to make me feel guilty, mad, sad, etc. or is it a legitimate request?" If it's legitimate, say "Yes" unless there's some very important reason for a "No." Be honest with your answer. For example, if one of your children asks for a bicycle, don't say "I can't afford it" unless it is true. Say "I don't want to spend the money that way," or "I worry about the heavy traffic on our street and don't want to risk your being hurt," or whatever the real reason is. Giving a child information is a good stroke (that will touch at least two of her or his ego states).

A child will feel safer if given facts rather than evasive statements and will also feel a sense of self-esteem because you have trusted him or her with the truth.

*"OK Muriel, I can see how that is with something like a bicycle request, but some things shouldn't be talked about with children."*

What do you mean, some things? Do you mean money, or impending divorce? If so, then I disagree. By the time they are school-age, your children have developed an Adult ego state, capable of objective reasoning. They need to learn about money, sex, divorce, and other important aspects of life from you. ❧

Take money for example. I believe in *earned* allowances,
and lots of fun small gifts like ice cream cones and
merry-go-round rides. Some people believe that children should get money just because they are part of the
family. But dad doesn't and neither does mom. Of
course there are times in any home when everyone
needs to pitch in and help, but in the real world, unless
you're on relief, you work for your money. The importance of this can be learned in the home, and the chores
and payment can be tailored to the age of the child.

My children are grown up now, so one of the things
I do is to have a group home for six foster children—all
girls—between the ages of ten and fifteen.

Each receives a monthly clothing allowance of $20
that they spend on clothing any way they choose.
Since the money must cover all their clothes, it requires
careful shopping, and the girls have learned to shop
very well. The budget for rent, food, phone, etc. is
also explained to them. Because they have this information, money "hassles" seldom occur.

Household chores are done on a rotating basis and a
fair allowance is also paid for doing them. Occasionally the girls trade or "sell" their jobs to each other;
one may not want to do something, another may want
additional money. This seems OK to me. Each learns
something from the transaction. If an unusual job
turns up, they all pitch in to get it done, or a fee is
paid to the girl or girls who want to do it. Now you
may not agree with the way I'm teaching them to
handle money, but it does work. So if you're having
difficulty along these lines, give it some thought. ❧

The kind of information given at the time of a divorce needs to be carefully thought through. Children need information given in such a way that they do not have to "take sides" against one or the other or do not become overburdened with their parent's unhappiness. They also need reassurance because they may be very frightened. They may intuit that the parent who is moving out may be severing parental ties with them. They may even think that it's their fault—that if they'd just behaved better or tried harder mom or dad would not be leaving.

I wish people who get a divorce would try to get a friendly one, but as a marriage and family counselor I have seen few of that kind. Usually one person wants it and the other is hurt, horrified, and angry at the prospect of being alone. Bitterness and sarcasm are common, and the friendship that may have existed between the couple at one time is seriously damaged. Children become aware of this and often feel torn apart with conflicting loyalties.

I was about 12 years old when my parents were divorced. It was a terrifying, lonely experience for me because it was not talked about. I was very confused because I couldn't understand what was happening. I had never known anyone who was divorced or whose parents were divorced. In fact, I discovered it only by overhearing a phone conversation between my mother and grandmother. When I asked both my parents about it, each said, "You wouldn't understand, Muriel." Neither of them ever spoke negatively to or about the other, and it wasn't until a year later that I found out that my father was going to marry another woman. And sure enough, I didn't understand. I was lonely and heartbroken because to me our family had been a happy one.

Because my dad was a university professor of dentistry, he had extended vacations each summer. So we would go on long camping trips, usually up into the High Sierras of Northern California—my mom, my dad, my brother and sister, our beautiful sheepdog Firpo, and myself. We would take a tent, folding cots, and cooking utensils (which I still have and use), pile ourselves and our equipment into a big old car, and head for the mountains about June 10th of each year. We learned to take care of ourselves, to cook outside, to fight forest fires if necessary, and to appreciate the beauty of the earth, the waters, and the skies. And it was great!

During the rest of the year the high point of each day was as dinner was cooking and we gathered around the piano to sing. Both mom and dad knew and loved classical music. Both were superb pianists and I can still see them playing from the green and black book we used to sing from most often. It was a condensation of many operas and we learned all the parts, solo and chorus. These were warm, happy times shattered by a divorce, and I suddenly felt very unsafe.

It was then, with my saved up allowance, that I bought what I used to call "my princess coat." It was a soft black cashmere fitted coat with a stand-up white fur collar (probably rabbit). I thought I looked like a princess in it and that I was supposed to look that way. I got that idea because, when I was younger and going out to something important, I would first go to my parents for a comment on my appearance. My mom would usually say, "You're lovely." My dad would usually say, "If you act as nice as you look, you'll be a princess."

So I got my princess coat when I was lonely and there was no one who would really talk to me. We lived in San Francisco at that time, west of Twin Peaks, and I remember that one day I put on my coat and took the K streetcar all the way downtown to the Ferry building and back while hoping desperately that someone would think I was a princess in disguise and talk to me. I was surprised when nobody did, and I felt confused. So I designed another plan. The next day I put on my princess coat again, got on the streetcar again, but with one big difference. This time I limped. "Surely," said my inner Child, "someone will notice me and talk to me." But no one did.

Now my Adult had new data. It was that clothes do not make a princess and clothes do not really fool anyone. Of course, I did not realize then that being a princess comes when physical and safety needs are met, when love and belongingness exist, when self-esteem and esteem from others lead a person toward self-actualization. The deep loneliness stayed with me a long time and it was many years before I began to feel like a princess again.

Enough about me for now. How do your children experience loneliness? If not by divorce, then how? And what about you? Are there some contracts you could make so that each of you would get and give more positive strokes that would take away some of the hurt?

Would you be willing to think about it? Now? Please say "Yes." Everyone in your family is important, and loneliness can be a terrifying, confusing, froggy feeling. So how about a picnic tonight. Outside if the weather is nice; inside on the floor on a red checkered tablecloth if it's too cold or rainy. Your home doesn't need to be unhappy. You don't need to go outside to play (as you may have been taught). If you look for joy, even in the midst of unhappiness you can find it. Have fun. Stay close. Love one another.

# Stepparents Step Carefully

Chapter 6

You've been divorced a couple of years. Been dating a little but not too happily. It's often hard to get a baby sitter and when you do the sitter sometimes has to be home early, often on the night you think you might want to stay late at someone's apartment.

Or, just as you get ready to go to a party your two-year-old starts coughing, her face looks flushed and feels warm. You want to go out but will feel guilty if you do and resentful if you don't.

Or, you've been dating someone new and exciting and then discovered he or she was really married, with two children of their own, looking for a brief affair rather than the stable relationship that you'd prefer.

Or, you're seriously thinking of marrying someone but he pays more child support for his two children than you receive for your two. He may also want to spend a lot of time with them and sometimes you feel jealous because your ex-spouse can't be counted on to see your children regularly. He's dating someone else and goes skiing with her on weekends.

Or, you're thinking of marrying someone who is very attractive herself, but actually is not the good house-keeper your ex-wife and mother both were. You tend to be pretty tidy, and wonder if that could be a bone of contention later.

Or, you're thinking of marrying someone and everything is great between you but actually you'd just as soon not have his or her kids around. You want the freedom from raising kids, not the burden.

But you do want to get married because living without a partner has too many lonesome moments.  Sure you can date but somehow that isn't quite enough.  Besides, it's beginning to feel as though you're in love with a particular person who is understanding and fun to be with.  It's someone you can talk to without being put down; someone who seems to appreciate you for who you are; someone who strokes you with those good 18 carat gold feelings.  And so, to marry or not to marry, that's the question. ❧

Now, don't skip the following section if you're not a stepparent. *It has some important stuff in it for any kind of parent or anyone who is thinking of becoming a parent—step or otherwise.* Some of the ideas will surely make sense to you no matter what your relation to children is or will be. They'll trigger off some new insights that might be very useful.

*"Well, I know enough to know that I don't know it all, Muriel, so go ahead."*

OK. Let's start with the Parent ego states of you and this person you're married to or might marry. The reason for starting there is to see if these two ego states are compatible. It's fairly important to know. If they are, you're miles ahead. If they're not, you will need to be very much aware of the areas of disagreement and have techniques to deal with them. When rearing children, people tend to act from their Parent ego state with attitudes and behavior copied from their own parent figures. So ask yourself this hypothetical question: "If my parent had been married to his or her parents, instead of to each other, how would they have gotten along? As a married couple? As parents? What would they have disagreed on?

You see, when people marry each other they have an Adult–Adult legal contract—but their Parent ego states get married too, as well as the inner Child. So look at the following figure and try to imagine how *your mother* would get along with his or her father and how *your father* would get along with his or her mother.

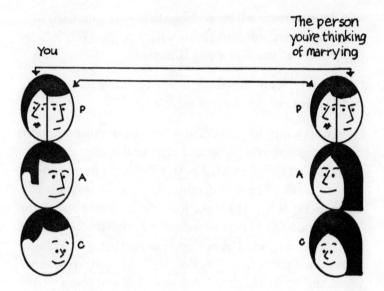

For example, if your mother thought it was OK for children to be noisy and the other person's father thought children should be seen but not heard, you are likely to disagree on how noisy the children should be.

Or, as another example, if your father thought that children should work for what they get and the other person's mother was indulgent with money, you're likely to clash on chores, allowances, and spending money.

Whenever your psychic energy moves into your Parent ego state, as it is likely to do when you are parenting, you will copy your parents and their opinions for better and for worse. So list the areas of agreement and disagreement. Who will be strict and about what? Who will be lenient and about what? Figure out Adult procedures to use when you disagree.

*"Oh, wow, this makes it a whole new ball game, Muriel, and I'm not sure that I like what I see."*

Now wait a minute. Don't give up just because the odds may be against you. You can change them by deliberately creating a new Parent, a better Parent, a more rational loving Parent. You can do this by using your Adult. The process is to: (1) Make long detailed lists about the OK and not-OK things about your parents. (2) Observe good parenting, read about good parenting, go to classes about good parenting. (3) Consult with your own inner Child and other children. Ask yourself and them what they feel would make a good parent. (4) Now that you have a lot of data, decide what kind of new parent to be and decide what to do. (5) Practice and keep practicing this new behavior. It will be using your Adult.

At first the new behavior may seem awkward, phoney, and uncomfortable. New things often do. If you keep working on it, however, the day will come when you *automatically* respond in these new ways, automatically use different and better responses than those of your own parents. When this happens you will have a new Parent in your ego state. The process would be like that shown in this figure. The last part of the figure shows what the ego states would be like in an eight-year-old child who has good parents or whose parents have developed new Parent ego states.

Eight-year-old child of a parent with a new parent

As a result of *your* developing a new Parent, your *childrens'* Parent ego state will be more caring, their Adult will think more clearly, and their Child will feel good. This will also be true for you.

*"Well, OK, but can you give me an example of how that might work?"*

Yes, out of my own experience, which was something like this. Although, my mother and father were very caring, responsible parents in many ways, I cannot remember if they ever *asked* me how I felt (they probably told me how they thought I was *supposed* to feel). Nor did they ever touch me, so far as I can remember.

Some years ago I decided, from my Adult, that they were wrong in rearing children that way. My Child ego state probably pushed my Adult to make that decision. After all, children, including the Child in me, *do* want to be asked about their feelings and they *do* want to be touched and held. So I started asking people how they felt and started touching other people and my own children more. I also looked for friends who were warm and touching as well as friends who were interesting intellectually.

At first this new touching felt very uncomfortable, but in time it became automatic and formed part of my New Parent in my Parent ego state. Naturally it pleased my Child, and my Adult thought then—and still thinks—that it's a better way to be.

In fact, I tried this approach with my own mother. She was in the hospital with a bad case of flu. Our relationship had always been friendly but rather formal and distant. I wondered if I could use my new skills and insight to minimize the distance and to increase the affection. So my Adult made up a plan and carried it out.

What I did was to go to see her in the hospital five or six times a day, very briefly.  I would stay just a few minutes but instead of sitting on a chair beside the bed, I would sit close to her on the edge of the bed.  I would also go up and pat her on the arm or on the cheek each time I entered or left the room.  In the beginning I felt her shrink back.  After all, this was as new for her as for me, and she had grown up in a rather formal situation.  I didn't comment on my touching, nor did she.  We talked superficially about the weather, the hospital, the children, and so on.  After a few days, instead of just a light touch with my hand, I would give her a little kiss on the side of her face, each time when I came in and each time when I left.

Then one day I decided to test it out.  I did not touch her and sat on a chair instead of the bed.  Suddenly Mother reached out her arms to me and said, "Oh, Muriel, come sit here by me."  And I did.  And she stroked my arm and murmured, "I'm so glad you're you."  And I was glad I was me.  It was such a beautiful unconditional stroke that much of the Grand Canyon feeling of loneliness was filled up at that moment.  And the feeling was very, very good.  The New Parent in me had parented my own mother, and she had loved me back.  Wow! ❧

Now, you may be dead set against touching or against giving compliments verbally. If you are, think about it some more. How will your children, your stepchildren, or your spouse know you care if you don't show them or tell them? Working hard to bring home the bacon or keeping the floors polished isn't enough. Everyone needs genuine compliments and positive strokes.

*"All right, Muriel, I'll do some more thinking about more stroking. But now will you apply that concept more specifically to second marriages?"*

Of course. Let's suppose that you haven't yet tied the knot, you have children by your first marriage, you're thinking of getting married again, and you're wondering how effective this other person would be as a stepparent. You already know, though you may not want to admit it, even to yourself, that what goes on between the two of you during your courtship may or may not continue when there are children around. If your courtship is Child-to-Child fun rather than Adult-to-Adult problem -solving, married life might not be as interesting or as exciting. But plug in your Adult and ask one of the most important questions, "Does this person need to develop a new Parent? If so, would this person be willing to do it?

*"Good questions, Muriel. And how do I get the answers?"*

First, *listen* as this particular man or woman talks about children. Is it with sarcasm? Bitterness? Understanding? Affection? Respect? Also, watch and listen if this person has children. What are they all like when

they're together?  Then ask yourself about the two sets
of children, how will they get along?  Watch and you'll
know more about that person as a parent.  People are
what they do.

Then, if you're planning to be a stepparent, evaluate yourself.  How might you do?  Do you really like those
other children?  If not, you're in for a lot of unhappiness.
You'll be critical, impatient, maybe even jealous and
angry.  Even when children and parents are at odds there
usually is a strong loyalty between them that will resist
criticism from an "outsider," and that's what you'll be
for a long time.  You'll need to *earn* love and appreciation from the children.  You'll need to *prove* that you're
trustworthy and rational, rather than unpredictable and
irrational.  You will need to *work hard* on it, because
children want to think the best of their own parents no
matter what.  And you will be a threat.  Therefore, step
gently.  When giving advice, walk as though on eggs.
Let discipline about homework, chores, money, clothes,
etc. be in the hands of the natural parent.

The truth is that the word stepparent has froggy connotations to many children.  This is because so many stories portray stepparents as cruel witches or evil ogres instead of wise, warm, wonderful kings and queens.
It certainly will be easier for you to win your step children's affection if you do have a wise, warm, wonderful king or queen as a parent in your Parent ego state.  But if you don't, you can create a new Parent with the ability to turn a froggy child into a prince or princess.

You will need to be especially careful about stroking. You will need to give out with lots of warm, fuzzy, positive strokes and hold back the cold, prickly kind.[8]

Sometimes it may be hard to do.  The Child ego state in you may be angry, tired, worried, sick, or anxious. It may want its own way *now*, without compromise. But as a stepparent or a parent, you'll need to compromise time and time again.  Even when you're angry, tired, worried, sick, or anxious you will need to wisely decide (like a wise king or queen) to be wonderfully warm (like a wonderfully warm king or queen) and to compromise.  You'll need to settle for humanness and not search for perfection—in you, your spouse, your children, your stepchildren or anyone else. ✄

*"OK, that's clear, even if it may not be easy. But what about the inlaws."*

What about them? You may be compared favorably or unfavorably. They may be upset because of their grandchildren's broken home and new stepparent. If so, give them time. They're human too. Furthermore, they're in your spouse's Parent ego state, so learn how to get along with them. Learn what kinds of strokes they hope for and give them a few.

*"Well, I guess I can do that, Muriel. But, say, what about the ex-partner and when the children go to visit him or her?"*

No matter how you feel, don't criticize the ex-partner. You probably are hearing only one side of the situation anyway, so withhold your judgment. One of the characteristics of a Child ego state is its intuitive wisdom about people. Your children have this childlike wisdom. Therefore, unless they are in danger when visiting the ex-partner, let them decide the pros and cons for themselves.

If they've had a bad time when visiting, create the kind of atmosphere that is healing. And don't be jealous if they've had a good time. The more good times, the better for everyone involved. Becoming a prince or princess is often due to the happy kingdom of home (or homes). Yours can be happy. ❧

The most common subjects of argument between parents or stepparents are money, sex, and how to raise children. We talked earlier about money and the need to give children factual information as soon as they are old enough to understand. Discussing sex, including anatomy, is also advisable. I well remember my ignorance when I was first married. At that time I evidently had never observed little boys' anatomy so I didn't know they had testicles. I was far too shy to ask my husband, "What is that?" and became more and more worried. Finally I went to my family doctor and told him we had a problem. He asked me to tell him about it, so I described what I called a "serious growth." Without cracking a smile my doctor said I must talk it over with my husband. I'm sure you can imagine how embarrassing it all was. Since then I've met several women with similar ignorance.

Some time later I approached my mother and asked why she hadn't told me more. "But, Muriel," she said, "You had an older brother and father and we weren't *that* modest. Besides, I used to take you to the museums a lot and there were many nude statues."

"Well, Mom," I replied, "Maybe they all had fig leaves on." ✄

When I think about the lack of Adult information and the misinformation that children get, it's not surprising that so many couples have sexual problems.

I personally believe children need accurate information about sexuality. Just before my third child was born, I was really big and used to joke about it a lot, saying things such as, "I'm getting so fat the baby is going to pop out of my ears." (At that time I didn't realize that children took things so literally.) One day I noted my six-year-old son walking around and around me, looking with puzzlement at my head. I asked him why. He said, "But Mama, it's going to be such a tiny, tiny baby to come out of one of your ears." Right then was the time for an anatomy lesson. ❧

Of equal importance is a child's need to develop healthy sexual attitudes. Seductive gestures or overtures, dirty jokes or snide remarks convey the message that sex is unclean or evil. Warmth, loving touch and respect for people of the opposite sex convey the message that sex is good.

Few children know details of their parents' sex life but most children pick up their parents' feelings and attitudes. The ways these are expressed are important messages that indicate laughter and joy or unhappiness and despair. When I was little, I remember my parents giggling in their bedroom. I didn't know exactly what was going on but it was clear, even to me, that they were enjoying each other. One of the finest gifts parents can give their children is a happy marriage. If one has failed, the second one doesn't have to.

If you are a parent or stepparent of a boy or girl in their early teens, you will need to be aware of the fact that as their bodies mature, their feelings go into a whirl and very small comments can trigger them off. Step particularly carefully at this time. Teenagers can outgrow their short tempers and tearful outbursts. They'll learn to love you for your tolerance and patience, and that's a very special fine thing to have happen.

Stepparents can provide stepchildren with a step up into a happier future. That's your challenge, your dream, your hope. You can do it. Would you be willing to think about it?

One of the things that will help you be more effective as a parent or stepparent is to learn what kinds of psychological games are played in your family and

what kind are played in your spouse's family—and learn
how to break them up in favor of more authentic living.
A game is a predictable pattern of moves, like those in
a card game or in a game of sports, that lead to a final
payoff. Everybody plays games but some play games
more often, or at a more intense level than others.

Games are learned in childhood. For example, a child
who often hears, "You stupid kid, you never do anything right" will learn to play the game of *Stupid,* doing
things wrong to provoke being called "stupid" once
more. Or a child who often hears "Shame on you"
will learn to play *Kick Me,* doing things wrong to provoke a psychological kick and a "shame on you" again.
The collected feeling—stamps discussed in a previous
chapter are the payoff at the end of a game. The game
is what is "played" to collect that feeling and is usually
played outside the player's awareness.

Whereas there are several techniques parents can use to
become aware of games in the family, the Game Plan
designed by John James is effective. To get the feel of
it, think about these questions. Have you noticed how
certain people in the family (including you) act in certain predictable ways and get certain predictable responses (the moves in the game)—and then end up with
predictable feelings that they usually have when things
go wrong (the payoff)? If you've noticed these things
happening, then you can identify patterns that will en-
able you to recognize family games.

To experiment with the Game Plan[9] think for a minute
about all the members of your family. See them in your
imagination. Then ask yourself the following questions
(if you write down the answers, the games will be more
evident to you):

- What keeps happening over and over again that
  leaves somebody feeling bad?
- How does it start?
- What happens next?
- Then what happens?
- How does it end?
- How do you feel then?
- What do you say to yourself at this point?

Now think of something else that keeps happening over
and over again. The feeling you collect at the end is
your psychological trading stamp. What you say to
yourself is a reinforcement of your OK or not-OK
feelings.

Use the same questions and see another Game Plan
emerge. Try it next from the viewpoint of your spouse.
What would he or she say? Or from your children's per-
spective—what would they say? Keep in mind that when
people play games they are seldom fully aware of what
they are doing. It takes two or more to play, so start
by breaking up your part in the game.

Ask yourself what you could do differently at each
point in the game. You may feel you've tried everything, but think again and list some possible new responses or what you could have done differently so the
game wouldn't have been played at all. If you have the

family council plan in operation, then you could try the question with everyone involved, "What keeps happening to you over and over again in this family?"

If you have a blackboard, you could jot down in brief phrases what it is that keeps happening, how it starts, what happens next, how it ends, and how people feel at the end. Then each person could think about what he or she could do differently so that the family could be more like a happy kingdom instead of a frog pond. You will need to look very closely at the points where stepparents and stepchildren are involved so that you can be sure that no one is being "expected" to play a froggy role. 🐾

One alternative procedure that you could use to replace bad games and bad feelings with good fun and good feelings is called "Upsetting the Apple Cart," because it gets rid of rotten-apple feelings that somebody is trying to collect.

The procedure for doing this is to give an unexpected response. For example, if one of your children is playing *Kick Me* by spilling milk on the floor, you can avoid rescuing him by cleaning it up and you can avoid persecuting him by yelling at him. Instead you can hand him a sponge and say firmly, "Now you can clean it up." This upsets the apple cart because your unexpected Adult response is likely to elicit a good feeling rather than a rotten one.

Or, as another example, if one of your children plays *Poor Me,* (I wasn't invited to the party), and if you usually say persecuting things such as, "Well, it's not my fault" or rescuing things such as, "Well, let's go get a milkshake and forget it all," you could upset the apple cart by saying, "Yes, it really is too bad," and to back to reading your paper. In this case your child would not get the expected payoff so the game would be broken up.

*"That's OK if it works, Muriel, but I don't think that kind of response would work with my children. Besides, it seems kind of gamey itself."*

Well, if it seems that way, or if you think it won't work, then don't do it. There are five other ways that families can spend time together instead of playing psychological games. These other ways are to withdraw or to engage in rituals, pastimes, activities, and intimacy.

When people withdraw psychologically from others, they are not really there. They may nod, smile, even carry on a conversation, but their thoughts are somewhere else.

When they are involved in rituals, they use simple stereotyped phrases such as "Hello," "Hello," "How are you?" "Fine."

Pastimes are much like extended rituals. When engaged in pastimes, people talk about safe subjects such as the weather. Their conversation is at a relatively superficial level.

(Both rituals and pastimes provide the people involved with minimal verbal strokes of recognition. These are necessary. So whenever people come together, rituals and pastimes often precede an activity of some kind.)

Activities are what people do that is usually thought of as work. They can bring people together or can separate them. Many activities in the home are carried out on an individual basis, like when Mom cooks and Dad mows the lawn. Each is doing something useful that benefits the family as a whole but that is not the

same as doing something together. Setting the table together is an activity that can bring people closer to each
other. So is working together on the budget or on a
homework project.

Togetherness is a necessary condition for intimacy.
When intimacy happens, it is usually in the middle of a
shared activity. For the moment, the Child ego states
of those involved are in a candid, game-free relation. ❧

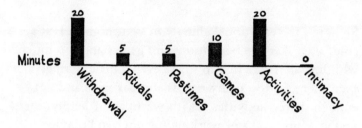

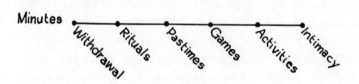

*"OK, we've got six different ways people spend time: withdrawal, rituals, pastimes, uh, games, activities, and intimacy. So?"*

So if you're interested, you can make a Time-O-Gram and graph the way you recently used one hour of your time. It might look like the top figure. Now, think of a three-hour period you recently spent at home. Out of that 180 minutes, how many minutes did you use in each of the six ways people structure their time? For example, did you spend 60 minutes physically present but emotionally withdrawn from the family as in reading, watching TV, etc.? Then what did you do with the other 120 minutes? In the bottom figure, mark the number of minutes above the line for each category. Then draw a vertical bar representing the minutes spent in each category. Do you like what you see?

So how's the emotional climate in your home? If it's cold, then there've been too many games and too much withdrawal. If it's just so-so, or even a little boring, then there are too many rituals and pastimes and not enough shared activities. If it's warm and friendly, then you've found ways of working together and playing together. And you know it and it's good.

It's hard to be a stepparent. It's almost as hard as being a stepchild. So continue to ask yourself, "What keeps happening over and over again?" If it's a game that ends with someone feeling bad, break it up. If it's activity and intimacy that leaves people feeling good, you can plan for it to keep on happening, over and over.

Again, it's fun to be a wise, wonderful, warm king or queen, and it's a super-stroke, to you and to them, when your little prince or princess emerges. ❧

# Home Is Where the Heart Is

## Chapter 7

You're at a luncheon with friends from high school days and the conversation turns to children. Two of the people across from you start to complain about theirs. The person to your left starts to brag about her daughter who got perfect grades, or the lead in a school play, or some other honors. It goes on and on and you begin to tune out and wonder when you can gracefully escape the chatter. Your seven-year-old comes to mind with her shiny big eyes and shy loving smile. You wonder if she'll get home from school before you arrive. And you hope not. Just last week she crawled up on your lap and said, "Mama, when you're not here, there isn't any heartbeat in the house."

You remember that you felt the same on the first day she went off to school. Something very precious was suddenly not there. Each moment that morning you had tried to imagine what her kindergarten class was like and your heart was with *her,* not with the housework and the phone calls, and the shopping. And you were oh so glad to see her when she came home with those big eyes, and shy smile, and spontaneous hug.

And you remember when your oldest son was called into the service and the empty feeling you got when you walked by his room, now so orderly in his absence, once so messy with his presence. And your heart reached out to him over the miles, and his reached back to you there at home.

And you remember when your husband was in the hospital and how the apartment seemed so incomplete without him. The clock didn't get set properly, the bills weren't paid on time, and the bed was oh so empty and still. Even a heating pad couldn't warm you up for your heart was really in the hospital, his "home" until he got well.

And you recall how your younger son asked for cookies when away at Scout camp. "Just so I'll know you're there," he grinned, and how at the same time he had offered, "Dad, I'll help you cut the wood. We men have to help out. We gotta keep the home fires burning."

Memory after memory, picture after picture of the family runs through your mind as you nibble on the creamed chicken and try to listen to the others talking about their families. But your heart isn't really there; it's flown home to meet your daughter and your body does likewise as fast as you can say goodbye to your friends. And you take a deep breath and you smile as you meet her coming in the door and you say, "Let's cook something good today as a special treat for daddy." And she looks at you and knows you care, and it's very good. And it feels like home.

Or, if you're a dad instead of a mom, you may be at your desk looking at a picture of your family, waiting for the clock to say 5 p.m. You dread it because it means facing the commuter traffic and you anticipate it because it means you'll be home, eventually, and you're glad of that. ❧

Speaking of home, think for a moment of the many ways people talk about it. Some people say they hate to go home, children as well as parents. For them it is a battlefield for expending emotions or a vacuum without warmth.

Some people make themselves right at home, children as well as parents, because it's comfortable and accepting.

Some people can hardly wait to get home, children as well as parents, because it's a refuge and a retreat from a hectic world.

Some people can hardly wait to leave home, children as well as parents, because it's unhappy or dull and uninteresting.

If you and your children try to define the word "home," what phrases or words would you use? Sit down together and make a list. Include everyone's ideas. Home to a child might be the smell of cookies in the oven, or the sound of Christmas music, or the lapping of waves on the beach, or wind in the trees, or the roses on the fence or the whistle of a train, or the barking of dogs, or the round dining room table, or the old oriental rug.

Talk about the people you know and the places you've been where you've felt at home. Expand your list. Then look it over and see if it was thought of as a "people-place" or as a "place-place." Talk about what might need changing and how the changing could be done.

If you think of home as a place, then your heart may be tied to a particular city, town, mountain, flat land, orchard, ranch, apartment or house. This special place may be like home to you because it feels familiar (like old shoes). When you go back to this place, or to a similar place, it is likely to feel very comfortable to you. Your Child ego state will be at ease if the original experiences there were happy.

One couple I know always fought over where to go for their vacation "home." In childhood each had had a home away from home. Hers was at grandma's beach cottage; his was father's hunting lodge. Neither was satisfied with the other person's concept.[10] Their hearts had different homes.

I remember once going to Brussels and being overwhelmed because of some small street that reminded me of downtown in my home town, San Francisco. I had a similar experience on a little street in Paris. The mountains of Arizona where my husband lived when he was little are like the Sierra Nevadas, where I camped all summer, so that I felt at home when visiting Arizona. Maybe one of the "cements" that keep us together is or preferences for similar geographical locations—big cities and high mountains. However, although my husband camped as a boy, he no longer enjoys it. "The army was enough," he says. ❧

I have lived in San Francisco or close by most of my life, and I love it. When I hear the nostalgic song "I Left My Heart in San Francisco," the memories it evokes are those of my childhood—Edgewood and Hillside Avenues (just off Parnassus), where I lived when I was very little; Santa Monica Way, where I lived at age six. Then Commodore Sloat School, where I felt stupid though people said I was bright; and Lowell High, where I struggled to get a ball in the basket during gym and was never able to. For three long years I never got the ball in the basket! And the Fairmont Hotel, where I sang with a dance band when I was a high school senior—until my father found out and insisted that I stop. "Nice girls," he said, "don't do things like that."

But you may have grown up in Los Angeles or New York or Kansas City, or some other place. For you, San Francisco may just be a city by a bay. Or perhaps you met someone that was important to you there or did something there that was exciting to you. The meanings each of us might attach to that one song might be different. On the other hand it might be "Sioux City Sue," "Going to Kansas City," "Do You Know the Way to San Jose?" "St. Louis Blues," or "Moon Over Miami" that turns you on because it reminds you of your childhood or some significant event since then. ✤

A geographical tie that feels like home is very important to many children and grown-ups. It strengthens them to cope with the continuing changes in modern civilization. So it's hard on many children when they have to move because their parents choose to or are forced to. Children may suddenly get attached to a substitute object, a favorite blanket or toy that represents "home" to them. Without this object they feel miserable themselves and are often miserable to be with. One little boy, whose parents moved from a one-story house to a two-story one, took his little chair with him and dragged it up and down stairs for months until he felt more at home.

*"Well sure, Muriel, but sooner or later everyone outgrows the nostalgia for home."*

Maybe they do, maybe not, but I remember when my mother moved. It was several years after I married but

I had lived in that pink stucco home, from age six until my wedding day. That particular house was "home" to me, so when I visited her, in her new home, I felt almost like a stranger. A few pieces of well-loved furniture helped put me at ease, but it was never quite the same. Now these same pieces of furniture, in the house where I currently live, remind me of my childhood and, for me, give the house a "homey" feeling.

The "home" for *your* heart may not be a piece of furniture or a geographical location; "home" may be represented by a person instead. A friend of mine, whose husband must move every year or two because of his job, trains her children to think that way with "Home is where we're all together with Daddy." However, I've noticed that although the focus is on Dad, this friend also has an important box of things that she always takes with her. An heirloom vase, a lovely picture, a few books, and some familiar knickknacks are lifted out of the box as soon as they enter the door of their new home. These simple treasures (things) seem to provide continuity and security. ✒

In summary, then, everyone's understanding of home is tied in with their childhood experiences—positive or negative. A child who is reared in a happy, warm, supportive environment will likely decide home is a good place, a safe place. The position he or she will take is, I'm OK and other people are OK. As this child grows up he will seek out friends who also came from happy, warm, supportive homes. When grown, he will develop his own happy home patterned after his childhood.

If a child is reared in an unhappy, brutal, emotionally cold, or depressing environment, that child is likely to conclude, I'm not-OK and other people are also not-OK. And, furthermore, home is not-OK. When growing up, such a person may make a conscious decision to create the type of home that is the opposite of what he or she grew up in and may be able to do so by sticking to the decision. But at times this same person may expect things to go wrong at home as they once did.

Now if the person from a happy home marries someone from a very unhappy home, some interesting disagreements can develop because their expectancies about a home will differ. For example, one may enjoy being home and being a "homebody"; the other may only enjoy going out for fun because he or she was not programmed to have fun at home. Their two Child ego states as well as their Parent ego states will be in conflict. They will need to analyze their differences, discover why they have them, and decide what they can do about them so that they will feel happy instead of

miserable. When this occurs, their home will become
a castle fit for kings and queens—and princes and
princesses. ❦

Shakespeare wrote, "All the world's a stage and all the men and women merely players." The home is the primary stage on which children learn what kind of a character they are expected to be and how they are supposed to play the part of frogginess or royalty. Each child unknowingly selects a psychological script (much like a theatrical script) which is based on early childhood experiences, especially those in the family.

It may seem strange to think of children acting out a drama unknowingly. To get a feeling for it, close your eyes, turn on your imagination, and look at the movie in front of you. See your home as a stage where some kind of drama is being performed. Watch what's going

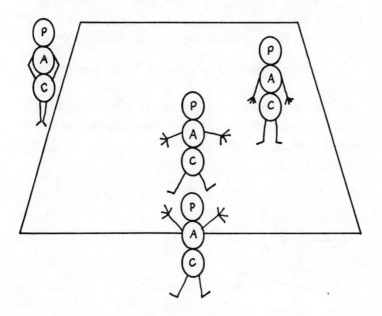

on. Then take a pencil and fill in, on the blank stage in the preceding figure, where each character might be positioned. Who's in the center of the stage? Is that person getting positive or negative attention? Are they getting it because of their behavior, appearance, age, or what? Is there competition for this place? Who's off to the side? Does that person like being there? Is someone completely off-stage—perhaps in the wings, giving stage instructions to others? Or out in front, directing the drama from an audience position? Or in a dressing room, sulking and refusing to play a part? And who is in the audience?

Now, in your imagination look again at your family drama as it is currently being played. Is it a comedy, an adventure, a tragedy, a melodrama, or what? Is it boring? Interesting? Funny? Tearful? Do you like your part? Do you think the children like theirs?

Every person is entitled to some of the spotlight. Are the people in your family taking turns? Or is one always the show-off and the others the supporting characters? If so, they need to be reprogrammed and re-scripted. ✤

The script is a result of a childhood search for answers
to basic questions: "Who am I?" "Where am I going?"
"What am I supposed to do?" "What happens to people
like me?" Eric Berne believed that children go around
having their various experiences, then one day when
hearing a fairy tale, children's story, or family legend
about someone like himself, a child suddenly concludes,
"That's me," and then copies the characters, dialogue,
plot, and action that he or she will use to play out a
unique drama in future life.[11]

A person who is able to recall their favorite fairy tale,
children's story, or family legend will get a glimpse of
the individual script being acted out. Children have
experiences, make decisions on the basis of the experiences, take psychological positions about themselves
and others, and select a script with behavior that rein-
forces their early decisions.

| Childhood experiences | → | Decisions | → | Psychological positions | → | Script-reinforcing behavior |
|---|---|---|---|---|---|---|

An example of this is the girl in the first chapter who
was often frightened. When she heard Jack and the
Beanstalk, and the giant who said, "Fi, fi, fo, fum"
she concluded, "That's me whose bones will be ground
up. Therefore, I'll hide." Hiding became part of her
script behavior.

Her childhood experience was being scared because she couldn't save her mother from her father's wrath. She chose then to identify with Jack and the Beanstalk. "That's me," she said to herself.

She then decided that people are not to be trusted and men are scarey and that it would be necessary to hide from them. Her psychological position was I'm not-OK and they're not-OK. And her script-reinforcing behavior was to select a spouse who would scare her with criticism and from whom she would try to hide.

Another example is the scripting process of a woman whose childhood experiences included her mother dying and her father then marrying a domineering, unloving woman. The fairytale she chose to identify with was Hansel and Gretel.

She decided that there was no one to trust except her brother and that she would stay away from people like father and stepmother. The psychological positions she took were we're not-OK (or mother wouldn't have died) and they're not-OK (mother for dying, stepmother for cruelty, father for indifference), therefore no one was OK, except her brother. This woman's script-reinforcing behavior was to marry someone like her brother, who couldn't really take care of her. Together they live an isolated life. They haven't been able to throw off the witch messages in their heads.

*"Well, Muriel, I just don't think I get it. Anyway, I can't remember a favorite story, so I don't see how your process could work for me."*

OK, try it this way: Think of some important childhood experience you had. Ask yourself these questions:

- What might a person who had that experience decide about themselves and their family?
- What psychological positions might they take?
- What scripty behavior might evolve that would, in some way, be similar to their childhood experience?

Or, if that still doesn't make sense to you, then skip the whole idea. One of the basic TA principles is to have a lot of options, so if one thing doesn't work you can try something else. Try one of these on for size:

- What happens to people like me who . . . ?
- If I go on as I now am, how will it all turn out?

Or, to get it closer to home, imagine what your children, stepchildren, or grandchildren will say about you after your death. Do you like what you think they'd say? If not, what will you need to do differently so they'll say something you'd like better?

If, on the basis of your childhood experiences, you decided to work hard to get affection, you probably feel not-OK unless you do work hard. So after your death they'll say, "Well, he (or she) sure did work hard," or your tombstone might say "She (he) tried."

What a eulogy!  I don't mean that it isn't **OK** to try things if the trying is really *experimenting* or *practicing*. But it's not so **OK** to just keep on trying instead of actually doing.  Princes and princesses and kings and queens are more than hard workers or people who "try." They do try, but they also enjoy life. ✢

How about you? And what kind of messages and experiences are you giving your children and how will these contribute to their scripts? I remember something my parents did that strongly affected my script. It was to "go see something," and San Francisco had a lot to see—a whale washed up on the beach, a big ship docked

at a pier, a new exhibit at the Museum, a building being torn down or put up. Almost anything was "something to go see," which we usually did on the spur of the moment. As a grown-up, I often find myself in the same pattern, doubting what I read in the newspapers, often having a strong urge to go see for myself—and usually doing so, on the spur of the moment.

Some parents, instead of giving positive encouragement and providing educational experiences, lose their tempers, and in fits of anger, scream such things as "Get lost," or "Get away from me and don't come near me again," or "I wish I'd never had you," or "You don't know the pain you caused me," or "You're going to turn out just like Uncle Harry (or Aunt Suzie) and you know what happened to him (her)," or "You just wait 'till you have children of your own," or "After all I've done for you." These kinds of comments are like a witch's curse.

Other parents, who also get angry at times, use their Adult ego state and say such things as "I don't like that," or "You'll need to learn not to do that," or "Stop it right now," or "Knock it off," or "Don't do it because . . . ," or "You know what you were supposed to do and you didn't do it. You also know the logical consequences, so . . ." These kinds of comments script children to know that they are responsible for their actions.

Some parents take care of their children physically but neglect other parenting functions. Other parents also take care of their children's physical needs but go a step further and teach them how to think.

Some parents want to be proud of their children but they act so their children are ashamed of them. Others want to be proud of their children and they set a good example for them to follow.

Some parents refuse to give their children positive strokes and compliments because they are afraid it will spoil them. Others give golden strokes lavishly, knowing that everyone is entitled to this kind of wealth in their own stroke bank.

My experience in working with thousands of parents, in parent training courses and in therapy groups, is that under all parental frustration is parental concern and love. And the problem is how to show the concern and love when one is frustrated beyond endurance, or when faced with problems that seem insurmountable.

In a nutshell, parents' problems seem to focus around the question of how to be wise, wonderful, and warm when feeling hateful, horrible, and hopeless, or how to give warm fuzzy strokes when receiving cold prickly ones, or how to royally "get on with it" when feeling stuck in the mud.

I know it isn't easy because I've been there, but the consequences for not getting on with it are less desirable than the struggle of actually doing it. ❧

*"Well doggone it, Muriel, what if I don't feel like getting on with it? Sometimes I get pretty damned tired of always trying, trying."*

Of course you do. We all do. That's human nature.

Well, there are three other choices besides "getting on with it."[12] I'll explain the four choices briefly, but if you want to read more about them or other parts of TA theory, I hope you'll refer to the bibliography at the back of the book.

The first choice, "Getting on with it," is the only one that stems from the position that I'm OK and you're OK: I'm OK and can do something about the problem and you're OK and will work with me on it. When my children were little and things were going well, I often felt everyone was OK. Those were good days and we "got on with it."

The second choice is to "get rid of." This is based on the psychological position that I'm OK and you're not-OK, so the message given is "Get lost," or "I'd like to be rid of you," or "You get in my way," When the teacher of my six-year-old was critical of him for his unbuttoned shirt, which she called sexually provocative, I felt that I was OK and he was OK, but the teacher wasn't, so I sewed the buttonholes to "get rid of" her.

The third choice is to "get away from." The psychological position for this is I'm not-OK (i.e., I never do anything right), you are OK (and do everything right). Therefore, I'll get away from you because I feel so inadequate around you. When in high school I couldn't even get the basketball in the basket, I felt not-OK and thought everyone else was fine. Then I wanted to "get away from" those others.

The fourth choice is to "get nowhere with." This emerges from the double not-OK position, I'm not OK and you're not-OK either. A person who chooses to "get nowhere with" believes no one can solve the problem, so why try? When my children were seriously ill, I had a double not-OK position. I felt like a not-OK mother for letting them get ill and I felt that the doctors were very not-OK because they either weren't available or couldn't provide instant cures. Those were hopeless "getting nowhere with" days. Now, even if things go wrong, I almost always choose to "get on with" them. I like the princess feeling. ❧

If you want to change your children's script or your own script, you will need to get on with it. You will need to change some of your childhood decisions. For example, if, as a child, you could never please your parents and consequently decided you'd never make it, you will need to redecide, "Even though I couldn't please my parents, I can make it, and will make it."

Or, if, as a child, you did not feel protected by your parents and made the decision that life was scary, you will need to redecide, "Life is not scary although my life sometimes has difficult problems that I need to solve."

The basic redecision many people need to make is to stop thinking, feeling, or acting like a frog and, instead, think and act like a prince or princess. If you do this consciously and deliberately, your froggy feelings will start to change. Eventually they will match your new prince or princess actions. You'll feel all together and it will feel good.

I remember when I used to be too froggy to make speeches in public. My knees would shake. If I had on high-heeled shoes, I would take them off, afraid that I would fall over if I left them on. I also stood behind a strong podium that would hold up the shaking me. Then, at age 35, I signed up as a university freshman. I decided for the first time to believe that I was not stupid, that I had something to say, that I could get approval without "putting on a performance," that I was going to speak without being scared, and that many people would be interested in what I had to say. And I did and I still do. And they were and they still are. And I feel good about it.

*"OK, Muriel, it sounds like it's worth a darned good try. But what about children? They're still in the process of deciding who they are and who other people are. How can they redecide when they're still making their original decisions?"*

That's just the point. They're still flexible, much more
so than they'll be in a few years. Because of their flex-
ibility, *now* is the time to act. Think about them.
Think about your home. Think about what's going on
between you. If something needs changing, then decide
to change it—now. Your whole pattern of stroking
your children may need changing. You may need to
give more conditional or more unconditional strokes.
But in either case, you will need to give them liberally.
Use the concept of positive reinforcement, which is to
give positive verbal or touch strokes for the kind of
Adult thinking that helps them to "get on with" life.
Also give verbal or touch strokes for the kind of child
fun and laughter that makes them a joy to be around.
Also give verbal or touch strokes for their Parent
nurturing that shows concern and responsibility for
others. 

The baby inside each one of us wants positive stroking
and unique kinds of positive stroking. Negative stroking
makes us feel like frogs, act like frogs, and treat others
like frogs. Because everybody at any age needs positive
stroking, everybody can contract to get it and give it.
This includes you and your children, me and mine.
Risk giving lots of positive strokes. What's the worst
thing that could happen if you did? Not much, huh?
Then what's the best thing? Let's go for that! <u>Now</u>
<u>that you've got'em, that's what to do with'em. Think</u>
<u>about it.</u> ❧

# A Further Thought

It's pretty well known that:
    What you give is what you get.

If you're a parent who gives wishy-washy strokes to
    children, you're likely to get wishy-washy strokes
    in return.

If you're a parent who gives critical strokes to children,
    you're likely to get critical strokes in return.

If you're a parent who gives warm, loving, golden
    strokes to children, you're likely to get warm,
    loving, golden strokes in return:
        —and hugs
            —and kisses
                —and more love

# Bibliography

For information on accredited Transactional Analysis therapists and educators and for information on other literature in Transactional Analysis write:

International Transactional Analysis Association
3155 College Ave.
Berkeley, Calif. 94705

For information regarding training or treatment in Transactional Analysis with Dr. Muriel James and Associates write:

Transactional Analysis Institute
Box 356
Lafayette, Calif. 94549

1. See Muriel James and Dorothy Jongeward, *Born to Win: Transactional Analysis with Gestalt Experiments* (Reading, Mass., Addison-Wesley, 1971) p. 36–37.
2. *Born to Win*, pp. 11, 242–244, 260–262.
3. Aaron Schiff and Jacqui Schiff, "Passivity," *Transactional Analysis Journal*, Jan. 1971.
4. Muriel James, *Born to Love: Transactional Analysis in the Church*, (Reading, Mass., Addison-Wesley, 1973) pp. 166–169.

5. Thanks to David Kupfer, M.D. for this idea.
6. *Born to Win,* pp. 188–190, 194–195, 214, 220.
7. See Abraham Maslow, *Toward a Psychology of Being* (New York, Van Nostrand, 1962) and *Motivation and Personality* (New York, Harper and Row, 1954)
8. Claude Steiner, "A Fairy Tale," *Transactional Analysis Bulletin* (Oct. 1970).
9. John James, "The Game Plan," *Transactional Analysis Journal* (Oct. 1973), pp. 146–149.
10. Cf. *Born to Win,* p. 158.
11. Eric Berne, *What Do You Say After You Say Hello?* (New York, Grove Press, 1972) p. 95.
12. Eric Berne, *Principles of Group Treatment* (New York, Oxford University Press, 1966), pp. 269–275.